conscious living

A collection of wholesome, plant-based and gluten-free recipes
to nourish your mind, body and soul

National Best-Selling Authors
Kelly Childs &
Erinn Weatherbie

Founders of the Award-Winning Kelly's Bake Shoppe

◆ FriesenPress

One Printers Way
Altona, MB R0G 0B0
Canada

www.friesenpress.com

Copyright © 2024 by Childs & Weatherbie Inc.
First Edition — 2024

All rights reserved.

No part of this publication may be reproduced in any form, or by any means, electronic or mechanical, including photocopying, recording, or any information browsing, storage, or retrieval system, without permission in writing from FriesenPress.

Cover and Photography by Suech & Beck.

Photos of Kelly & Erinn on pages: dedication, about this book, 6, 8, 13, 14, 23 by Maria Abramov

Photos on page 2, 18, 250, & Back Cover by Emilie Pelka

Photo of "Best Banana Bread" by Michael Nowacki

Food Styling by Lindsay Guscott

Prop Styling by Courtney Middleton

ISBN
978-1-03-913741-7 (Hardcover)
978-1-03-913740-0 (Paperback)
978-1-03-913742-4 (eBook)

1. COOKING, VEGETARIAN & VEGAN

Distributed to the trade by The Ingram Book Company

ERINN'S DEDICATION

For my love, Michael. I'm so grateful for our life together. xo

KELLY'S DEDICATION

I want to dedicate this book to the sovereign hearts and souls of all sentient beings in this world and to encourage us to believe in the love that connects us all. We are more than we think we are. This, sometimes difficult, evolutionary journey is for each of us to become immersed in the awareness of who we are and move into our compassionate, infinite, love frequency. It is all there is.

With love,
Kelly

Table of Contents

About This Book	1
Our Story	3
Part I: Living a Conscious Life	**11**
A Conscious Life and a Conscious Business	12
The Conscious Pantry	19
Superfoods	*20*
Conscious Grocery Shopping	*31*
Kitchen Tools	*36*

Part II: Recipes for Eating Consciously	**39**
Immunity Boosters	40
Beverages	43
Adaptogens	72
Smoothies and Smoothie Bowls	75
Breakfast	95
Fats	128
Entrees	131
Sauces, Sides, and Snacks	173
Plant-based Baking Essentials	200
Desserts	203
Conclusion	247
Acknowledgements	248
About the Authors	250
Additional Resources	251
Index	253

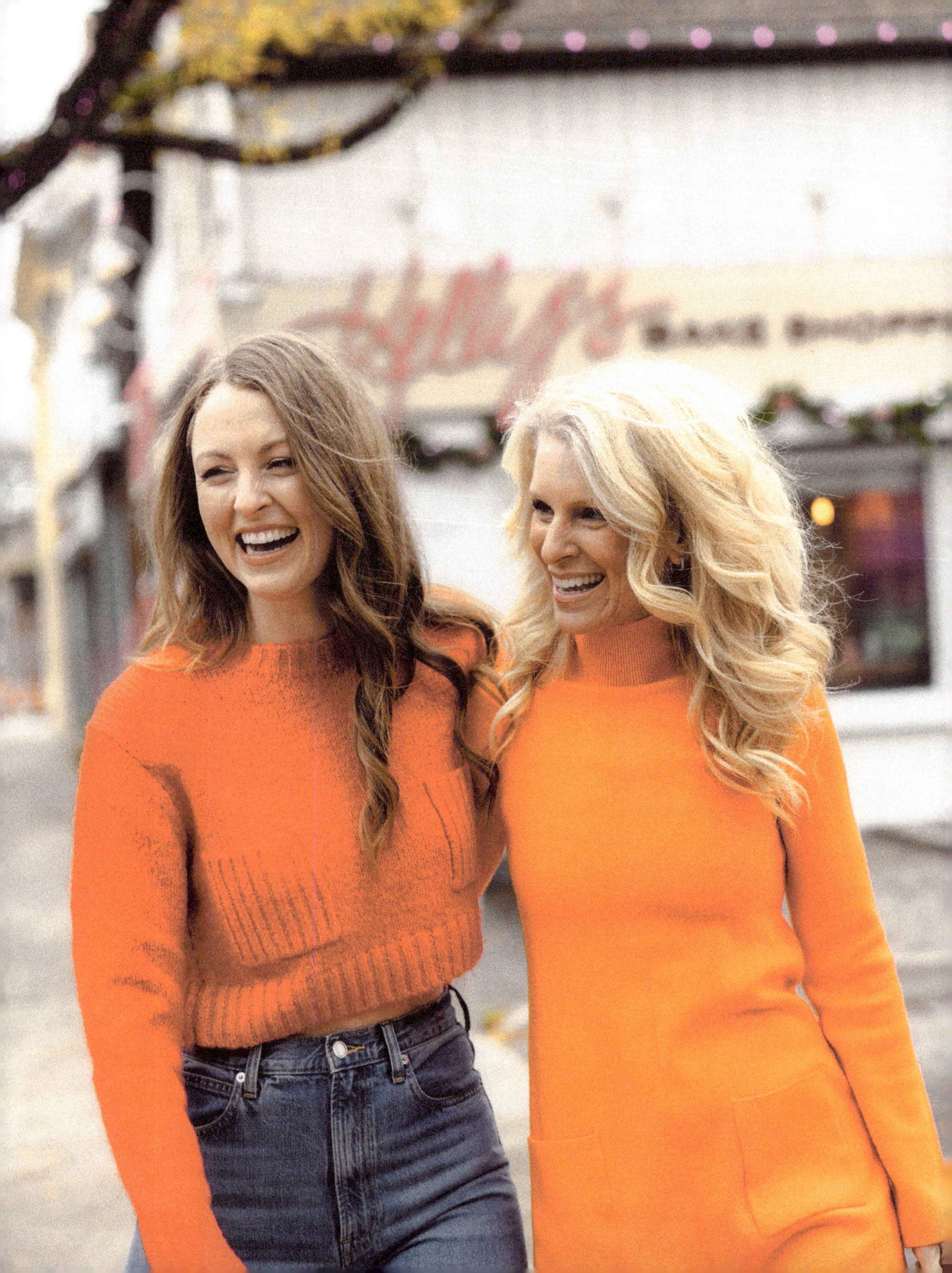

About This Book

Conscious Living is a book dedicated to giving you the tools and ideas necessary to live a more conscious life.

As a mother and daughter and business partners for over ten years, we see the need for showing up in our highest frequency and best selves possible on a daily basis for ourselves, our relationships, our business, and the world. Throughout this book, we'll show you how we've created a conscious life and business and share some of our favorite superfood recipes and mantras to help you live your best life ever.

SECTIONS

Conscious Living is broken down into two sections: The first is an introduction to conscious living, and the second is our recipes. Many of our recipes could fall into more than one chapter, so feel free to pick and choose from the various chapters to build your own meals.

OUR STORY & CONSCIOUS LIVING

In the early part of this book, we share our story and how we got to where we are today. We also share why conscious living is so important to us and how you can bring more consciousness into your daily life.

CONSCIOUS PANTRY

In our Conscious Pantry, we outline our kitchen staples and break down the key health benefits of each of these ingredients. We highlight what we deem to be superfoods and must-haves in the kitchen. While this list may not be exhaustive of everything we have in our kitchens, it is a very good starting point for the ingredients most often used in this book.

GROCERY LIST

Further into the Conscious Pantry, we outline our typical grocery list and break down the things that you'll need to make most of the recipes in this book.

INGREDIENTS

Almost all of the ingredients in this book are easily accessible in North America at your local grocery store, natural food market, or with a quick search online.

RECIPES

We encourage you to read the introduction for each recipe. Some of our recipes may require some advance preparation—like chilling certain ingredients or soaking nuts—so be sure to give yourself enough time. Also, we encourage you to experiment with making modifications to the recipes, but only after you've tried the recipe first the way it was meant to be made.

ALLERGIES

We are aware that many people suffer from allergies, and we have made our best effort to label any recipes that contain top allergens. All recipes are dairy-free, egg-free, and gluten-free; however, some may contain nuts and/or peanuts. If you are free of allergies, find your joy in swapping in your favorite ingredients to make a recipe your own. Everything at our business, Kelly's Bake Shoppe, is 100 percent gluten-free, dairy-free, egg-free, vegan, and peanut-free.

DYK

We have scattered "Did You Knows" (DYK) throughout the book to add a little insight into recipes and ingredients.

Our opening team at our 10th Anniversary of Kelly's Bake Shoppe

Our Story

Welcome to our world. We are Kelly and Erinn, mother and daughter, best friends, co-entrepreneurs, and honored to share this planet with you. We are so glad you're here.

Our mission has always been to bring a kind, passionate love and all-inclusiveness to the world, and somehow, it ended up in a bake shoppe.

We truly have been blessed with all that has manifested in our lives and in our evolution as souls figuring out our lives on this journey. One of our biggest takeaways is to always stay in a state of gratitude; we have come to realize that it changes *everything*. We truly mean it when we say, "Thank you for being here."

When we chose to adopt a plant-based diet in 2009, we wanted to share it with the world. We have always lived health first and optimally with whole, nutrient-dense foods but were never formally trained in pastry or culinary school; we just loved good food. So, when we opened our restaurant, Kindfood, in 2010, we realized immediately that we were blazing an exciting, new trail as vegan-restaurant pioneers in Canada. Kindfood—a restaurant, juice and smoothie bar, and bakery—was drawing folks from all over Southern Ontario and attracting attention across the country. The demand was undeniable. Incredibly, people were excited to try a new wholesome way of eating. We incorporated delicious raw and whole-cooked, plant-based foods and inspiration from Californian chefs and restaurants and put our own spin on it all.

The bakery component of Kindfood was birthed in the back of the cafe, in a space approximately six by nine feet. That was all the space in which our business could afford to squeeze some baking. The rest of the business's footprint was used up by a juice and smoothie bar, cook tops, produce fridges, a freezer, and tables and chairs.

When we opened up the doors of our sweet little cafe in May 2010, we used spelt and multi-grain flours and all-natural ingredients for all our sourdough breads and baked goods. Boy, did that change fast! Week by week, we noticed more and more people coming in and asking for gluten-free options for our food and baked goods. That made us think: *How can you make gluten-free "optional," when wheat is an airborne allergen?* It's impossible for people with gluten allergies. So, we took a leap of divine faith. By the beginning of 2011, Kindfood was converted into a 100 percent gluten-free cafe. We were already egg-free and dairy-free due to being vegan, but now we'd created this mecca of nurturing, allergy-friendly foods. These baked goods took way more work, however. Unlike our savory café, in which we could simply toast gluten-free bread for a sandwich or to make gluten-free croutons, it took weeks and months to create delicious, moist, healthy, gluten-free baked goods. The challenge was real.

In these early days, Erinn was working part-time at the cafe and going to university full-time, and Kelly, as it turned out, became fully immersed (one hundred hours a week) in recipe-creation mode. Kelly spent many lonely hours, starting her days at 3:00 a.m. or 4:00 a.m., pursuing the ultimate gluten-free and vegan baked goods. On many of these early mornings, the hard-rock music of Metallica, Smashing Pumpkins, STP, and Def Leppard kept Kelly company as she baked. These days turned into weeks and months. Reflecting back on that time now, it feels like another lifetime, and to be honest, those were the best days.... We miss those days of creation.

Figuring out how to make gluten-free brownies is a good example to give you an idea of what was involved. Transitioning from a spelt brownie to a gluten-free brownie is not as simple as just swapping the flours out. It is a true challenge. Getting the right texture, flavor, moistness, denseness, and even color, took over six months to figure out. Adjusting flax meal or sweet potato and adding the ever-so-small addition of espresso made all the difference in the world. Sometimes the brownie was too dry and would break apart, or too flat, too wet, not chocolatey enough, too chewy, or even go stale the next day. (Remember too, these recipe creations were all being done without eggs, butter, wheat flour, or conventional sugars. We were using only all-natural, nutritionally dense ingredients like flax meal, apple sauce, sweet potato, roasted bananas, pumpkin, etc.)

It all came down to praying for divine guidance (seriously), and one night, Kelly had a vivid dream that detailed what she needed to do to make the perfect brownie. When she awoke from this dream at 4:00 a.m., she knew she had to get to Kindfood as soon as possible, so that she wouldn't forget the process she had dreamed about. It was a cold, snowy, still morning, and as Kelly walked to the restaurant, something felt very different. Arriving at the front door of the business, she had to use her bare hands to dig away the snow to open the door. (The snow shovel had been left *inside*.) Once in the kitchen, Kelly carefully measured out all the ingredients and followed the instructions from the dream verbatim, writing down all the steps as she performed them. The brownie pan was put in the oven, and at the right time, pulled from the oven to cool.

When she tasted one of the brownies, the tears began to flow, and at that moment, the sun, moon, and stars collided. Kelly knew, deep within her core, that this brownie would change lives. It was "perfection." The instructions Kelly received from her divine dream worked. (Of course, it did!) The perfect gluten-free vegan brownie was born, and ten years later, it is still with us. This iconic, award-winning brownie recipe has never been altered, and it is still what makes Kelly's Bake Shoppe famous thanks to its deliciousness—not to mention the gluten-free, dairy-free, egg-free, vegan, peanut-free, healthy ingredients. To sum up, we'd just made the perfect allergy-friendly vegan brownie (and other baked goods).

The demand for our baked goods in those early days grew so rapidly that we had to move the bakery out of Kindfood. The decision to do this was another divine decision. Every day, Kelly and Erinn's treats sold out. Every day, we baked more and more and had nowhere left to go within Kindfood. There were many days when all horizontal surfaces (including customer tables) were treated as cooling racks and had cupcake and cookie trays on them. We simply ran out of space.

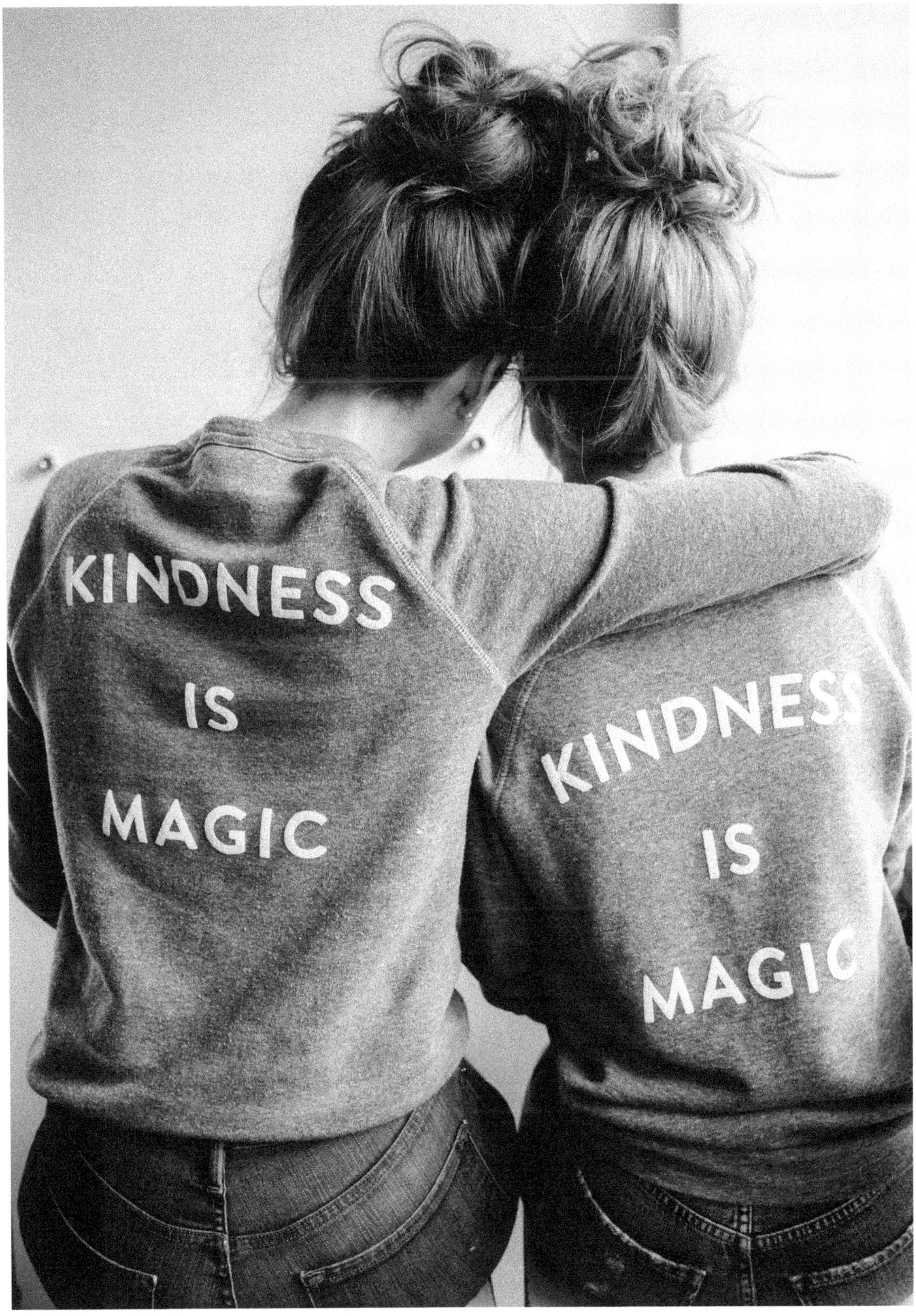
KINDNESS
IS
MAGIC
KINDNESS
IS
MAGIC

We're grateful for all of it. The highs. The Lows. The blessings. The Lessons. The setbacks. The comebacks. The love.

We clearly saw that the bakery was unique. The customers were always ecstatic and so grateful that we baked things for their children who would have otherwise missed out on these treats because of their allergies. They spread the word about who we were and what we did. Customers wanted cakes, cupcakes, cookies, and treats to share and celebrate with others. We were the catalyst in opening up the world for *all* people, regardless of their dietary restrictions, to celebrate memorable moments together. We did it all. We were gluten-free, dairy-free, egg-free, lactose-free, and then we'd decided to drop peanuts and nuts too.

Sweet treats are special and resonate on a different level than savory food in a restaurant. What we mean by this is that **cupcakes and treats bring joy!** They make everyone happy. Just like Willy Wonka's chocolate factory ignited a light in children's eyes, we knew we had the power to bring this joy into the world. We just knew it had to be done—even when some family members pooh-poohed our idea and said, "How will you pay your bills with cupcakes?" We trusted our passion. We realized this would be more than a bake shoppe; it would be a missing connection that people were dying to find. When parents started coming in with tears running down their faces because their son or daughter with allergies had just had their first brownie or were able to share a birthday cupcake with their buddies in their classroom, we knew we were on the right path. We felt our hearts swell and knew this bake shoppe would have its own heartbeat.

To much fanfare, Kelly's Bake Shoppe had its grand opening in downtown Burlington on December 7, 2012. The line-up of customers was down the street and still is to this day.

And now, after appearing on national television fourteen times and receiving front-page media news, being named number three on Buzzfeed's "Top 25 Sweet Cupcake Shops to Visit Before You Die," being showcased in *Hello! Canada Magazine*, and *Food & Drink;* receiving the Burlington Tourism Ambassador Award; and having a national best-selling cookbook and a staff of twenty-six, I'd say we have done okay.

Recently, we spent some time calculating how many people we have served and how many cupcakes we have baked since December 7, 2012. As of the time of this writing, we've baked over 1.5 million cookies, two million cupcakes, and endless brownies, and have served close to **2 million beautiful customers**. Kelly's Bake Shoppe is now in its tenth year. Sure, we have had to overcome a zillion things over the past couple of years, but the biggest lesson we have learned is to have faith that all will be well and that nothing else matters except for love. The connections we have with one another are what keeps us alive and thriving. We are honored to be loved and supported by so many. Please know that the feeling is mutual. We are honored to love you all back. We are honored that this business has provided a positive-energy space and enabled us to give back to the community every day. We have been able to sponsor high-school proms and sports teams and support palliative care, underprivileged schools, women's shelters, veterans' welfare, the SPCA and other animal welfare groups, water rights for all, Indigenous rights, Rainbow Railroad, BIPOC foundations, front-line workers, and Saving the Amazon. We have supported organizations for individuals with Down's syndrome and Autism. We even played Santa for children in low-income families, and on your birthday, are happy to offer free birthday cupcakes at Kelly's Bake Shoppe! The list goes on and on and on.

In April 2016, we published our first cookbook, *Made With Love,* with Penguin Random House. Within eighteen days, it was a national best-seller. We had the opportunity to tour the West Coast on a book tour and were treated like royalty on radio shows, podcasts, and TV interviews. It was truly an honor to receive this recognition.

Our beloved *Made With Love* cookbook (2016) has fifty sweet recipes and fifty savory ones from our restaurant, bake shoppe, and our lives at home. This *Conscious Living* cookbook carries on this tradition of sharing and reminding people that what is most important within humanity is LOVE. Love is all there is. When you create from love and compassion and give of your heart, you are always divinely guided and inspired.

Life is a journey, and it is our honor to share ours.

LOVE FOR KELLY'S BAKE SHOPPE!

"***Delightfully Delicious.*** *Kelly's Bake Shoppe is a gem in the confectionary industry. Their product is consistent and very tasty. As a person living with food intolerances, it is truly great to be able to enjoy treats made with special considerations in mind. This bakery has awesome brand recognition for being a small, family-owned business, and provides a nice mix of classic and new creations. I loved serving Kelly's at my wedding, and now to celebrate occasions with my children. Thanks for making life sweet."*

"***Nothing Short of Incredible!*** *As someone with allergies, Kelly's Bake Shoppe adds SO much joy into my life. It's my all-time favorite place to go. The treats are to die for, and worth every penny. The staff are incredible, the area is adorable, and the memories made here are unforgettable. 11/10 recommended!"*

—Nicole P.

"***Best baked (almost) guilt-free goods ever!*** *I have tried a wide variety of the menu items and even though I am not vegan, nor do I try to follow a vegan diet/ lifestyle, the Nanaimo bars and the snickerdoodle cookie sandwiches were the best baked goods I've ever had. One wouldn't even be able to notice that they were made with healthy, plant-based ingredients. I highly recommend!"*

—Kristen K.

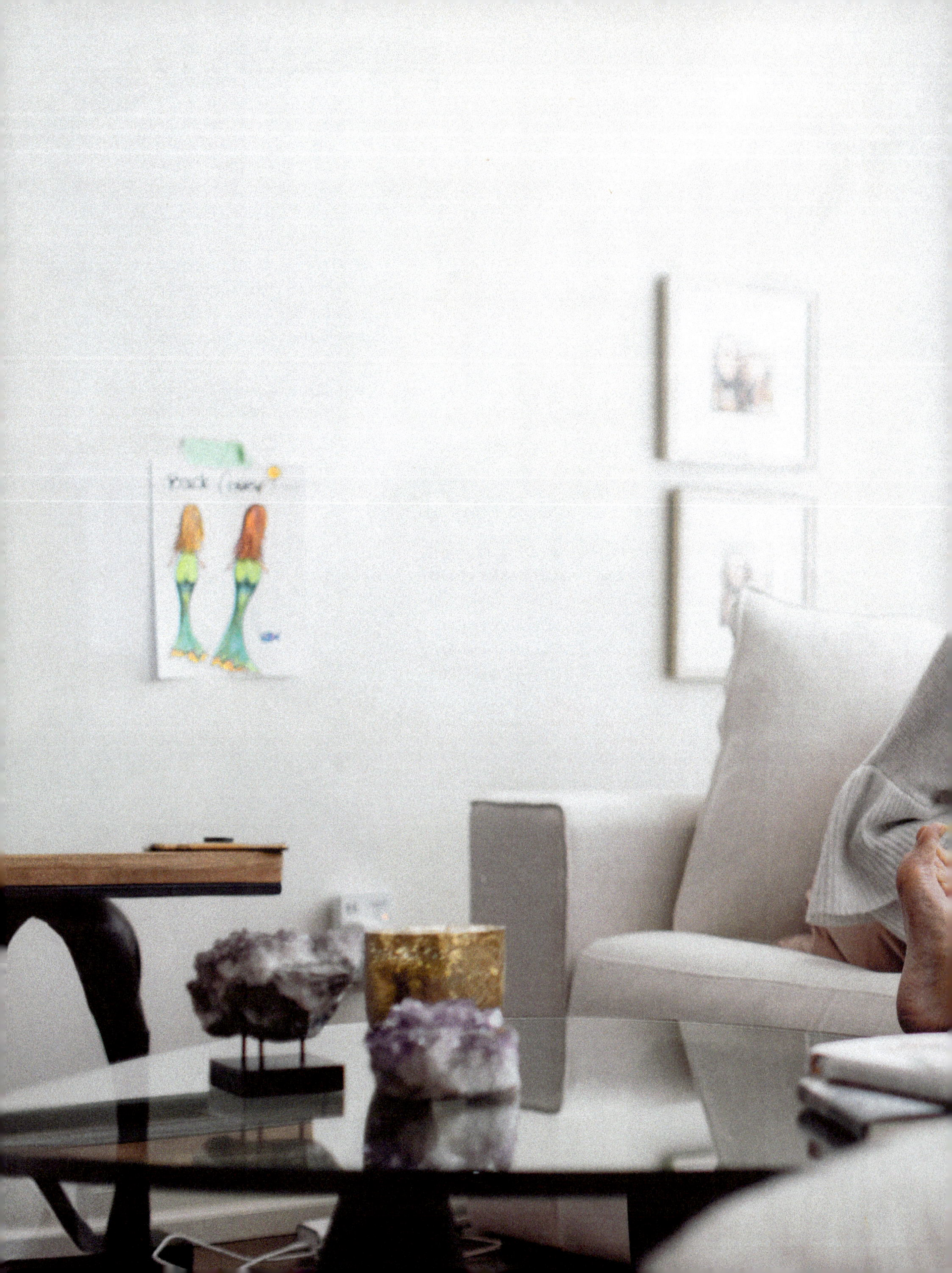

PART I
living a conscious life

A Conscious Life and a Conscious Business

Consciousness is the awareness of our experience of life. It is the awareness of the emotions that arise within us and our heartfelt truths and how we reflect them. Being conscious is embodied by eating only healthy, nutritious food to fuel the body's cells and being aware of and grateful for the things in our lives that bring us joy. Reflecting on our purpose in this lifetime can be truly transformational.

Over the past almost twelve years of being in business as Kelly's Bake Shoppe, we have done a lot of reflection on our personal lives and our business and have done our best to learn and grow spiritually. What we've come to realize is that all of the outside noise is explicitly designed with one purpose in mind: to distract you from what is currently happening to you as you develop as a person. If you manage to turn off the outside noise of the distractions, confusion, and even the mainstream media and simply tune into the stillness of your heart, you will find an energy source that will guide you through the pain, darkness, suffering, and chaos and into the light. This is called consciousness. Never forget that we are all far from perfect, but living with vulnerability, courage, gratitude, authenticity, and passion is what makes us wise.

So, how do we turn off the noise? It sounds easy, but it can be so difficult. It begins with setting the intention of creating a more loving, compassionate space for yourself. The intention is very important as it sets your energy to tune into that request. The Universe will respond and help you. We live with limited noise in our homes and make an effort to turn off electronic noise (TVs, music, social media) that can hijack the best of intentions. We find that our quiet morning and evening meditations—even if only for five minutes—are necessary to create our best possible days. The meditations could mean baking healthy and nurturing cookies in the kitchen, walking in nature and listening to the birds, or being aware of trees blowing in the wind. Know this: Even taking a warm bath with sea salt and essential oils can create miracles for your life. It begins with you taking that first step to connect in new ways to your life.

For us, awareness and consciousness within our lives means moving towards more joy because we intentionally surround ourselves with the people and things that ignite our hearts. We consciously choose to be aware of our reactions and emotions and feel our energy. Decisions in life and in business are done with purpose, and we visualize the outcome. It means greater health because we are aware of what we eat and choose to nurture the vessel of the soul. We know that what we eat "becomes" us, and that's why we have such passion for this book. Consciousness reduces stress as it brings awareness of who we are to the surface. We can then recognize the suffering caused by holding onto things that no longer serve us. How many of you have held onto thoughts about a situation or a person, and every time you think about it, you feel uncomfortable and angry? It is ridiculous how long we can hold on to these toxic feelings. In most situations, the person has no idea you are still hanging onto your angry thoughts, so who are you punishing?

A CONSCIOUS LIFE AND A CONSCIOUS BUSINESS | 13

the world says "you must hustle to succeed."
The soul whispers, "isn't there another way?"

- Ashmi

Our goal was to become more centered. How did we accomplish this? Well, the first thing we did was to take up meditation. This was truly a saving grace for us. We also introduced a life coach into our business that helped us to better communicate and exchange information, and to recognize each other's strengths within the business. We took up growing dahlias and vegetables, and we became mesmerized by watching the gorgeous blooming flowers, bursting with color, and the heirloom tomatoes, growing on their vines and morphing into colorful works of art. Yes, we achieved instant meditation in the garden.

Do you ever feel like the Universe is speaking to you? Do you ever feel like you get a nudge to step into a new aspect of your life? Maybe it is not a nudge. Maybe it's a gut punch. What do you do? Do you ignore it, make excuses, and shut the voice down? Do you sit with it and try to explore it more? Do you surrender to it with gratitude and thank God for the clarity? What would it take to make that step forward and release all the fear and resistance that is holding you back? Trust us; we know it can feel scary moving into uncharted waters, but simply tuning into calming music or getting to the nearest hiking trail can do wonders for elevated emotions.

We had a calling to open Kelly's Bake Shoppe. It wasn't a nudge; it was a profound gut punch. The miracle happened on a Saturday in April 2011, during a midday customer rush at Kindfood. Our bakery sales were out of sight! Customers were lined up to collect their orders, and the bakery business model was revealing itself right before our very eyes! Kelly was pretty passionate and yelled in classic Kelly fashion, "That's it! We are getting our own f***ing space and getting away from the onions and garlic in the (Kindfood) kitchen!"

It was pretty simple to be honest. Speaking your truth gives great clarity to all concerned. You might even be able to call it an undeniable shout from the heavens. What we were creating in our little bakery was needed by many. We could visualize it. We could "feel" it. And yes, of course, we could "taste" it too. There was, without a shadow of doubt, a true energetic synchronicity with the Universe. This decision was pure, natural, and flowed. This was our intuitive messenger waking us up to listen—and listen we did as the collective consciousness of everyone within Kindfood turned on. Then it was full steam ahead to find a location and build a magical space. Finally, in December 2012, we opened our doors to a line of people down the street. Filled with such gratitude for all this love, we have never looked back.

We were both beyond ecstatic as we had found what turned our souls "ON," and we didn't back down when other people projected *their* limitations upon us. That has a real effect on many. Focusing with clarity and visualizing a project, with your heart full of joy, can manifest so much in your life!

When we made the decision to open our business, we were scared but also full of adrenaline! Adrenaline isn't a bad thing because it keeps you wide awake and not needing too much sleep. It's scary: creating a business from your heart and exposing it to the world in a three-dimensional retail box. We would never be able to please everyone. Would we be loved and supported by enough people to pay our bills and make a living? Would we find staff and people who truly wanted to work for our business? We hoped that by creating a business filled with positive energy, we would call out to our tribe and find our connection with others. But nothing was guaranteed. All we knew was that the burning desire within us was going to push us forward.

Now, after a decade as a small business with an average of twenty-five to thirty staff at any given time, we have had the blessing of extraordinarily amazing times. But what is life without the challenges? Yes, like a lot of people, we also encountered multiple challenges both in business and in our personal lives over this span of time. What came from these challenges was nothing less than the miracle of pure, divine, personal growth. Was it painful? You betcha. At times, the hurt was so deep that sleeping was the only escape from the pain. Yet step by step, we journeyed forward. We meditated, prayed, and let go as best we could. We immersed ourselves in nature and trusted the divinity of all there is to guide us from the darkness. We found our strength in miracles that kept randomly landing in our laps: incredible people, brilliant consultants, beautiful emails, encouraging messages, and loving hearts that fell from nowhere.

We found a power deep within our hearts and shifted our whole perception of pain and our lives. We recognized how exceptionally blessed we were as we journeyed through life. No one can take that from us. We even found our strength to take on more and to put our heartfelt messages on the pages within this book.

One of our biggest lessons over the years has been that you can get lost in a business and the fanfare and allow it to consume you if you do not have clear boundaries. These boundaries are there for a reason: to help create a balance that protects the soul and one's creativity. A lack of boundaries results in an infringement into one's personal space. In complete transparency, it was really tough for us to implement these boundaries. Call it "tough love" if you will. When we grew to such a size that another layer of management had to be hired to enable us to grow the business to a higher level, it was like cutting ourselves off from our own child. But it needed to be done. We couldn't grow our business when we were so busy focusing on day-to-day procedures from the inside. We needed to ZOOM OUT to forty thousand feet to see the picture more clearly. We had to learn how to stand separately from the bake shoppe because we are *more than our business*. When people ask us who we are and what we do, we like to say this: "We are Kelly and Erinn ... best friends, visionaries for a kinder planet, and oh yeah, we also own a bake shoppe."

One thing we have realized over the course of the past ten years is that you cannot ever cancel love. No matter how hard the darkness may try to suppress you and take away your voice, no matter how adverse the conditions might be that hit you, love can never be destroyed. Abundance on all levels is your birthright. The world is in chaos. We know this. But in that chaos is pure magic because in our darkest, most painful times ... we can find the miracles in life. It is a journey. Never before has there been a more crucial time to connect compassionately with one another while standing in our own truth. Consciousness means we are always bringing ourselves back to our peaceful center of love, calmness, and joy. It then radiates outward to allow others to bask in it. No matter where we are or what may happen on this planet, we will always have our love for one another, for humanity, and for ourselves. LOVE. This is what is needed now more than anything else.

May we all connect with our love tribe.

Love,
Kelly & Erinn xo

"Be that dawning sun upon the earth. Don't wait for the earth to shine on you. The earth is not there to light you. You are already lit. YOU are the light to the earth."

—*Anonymous*

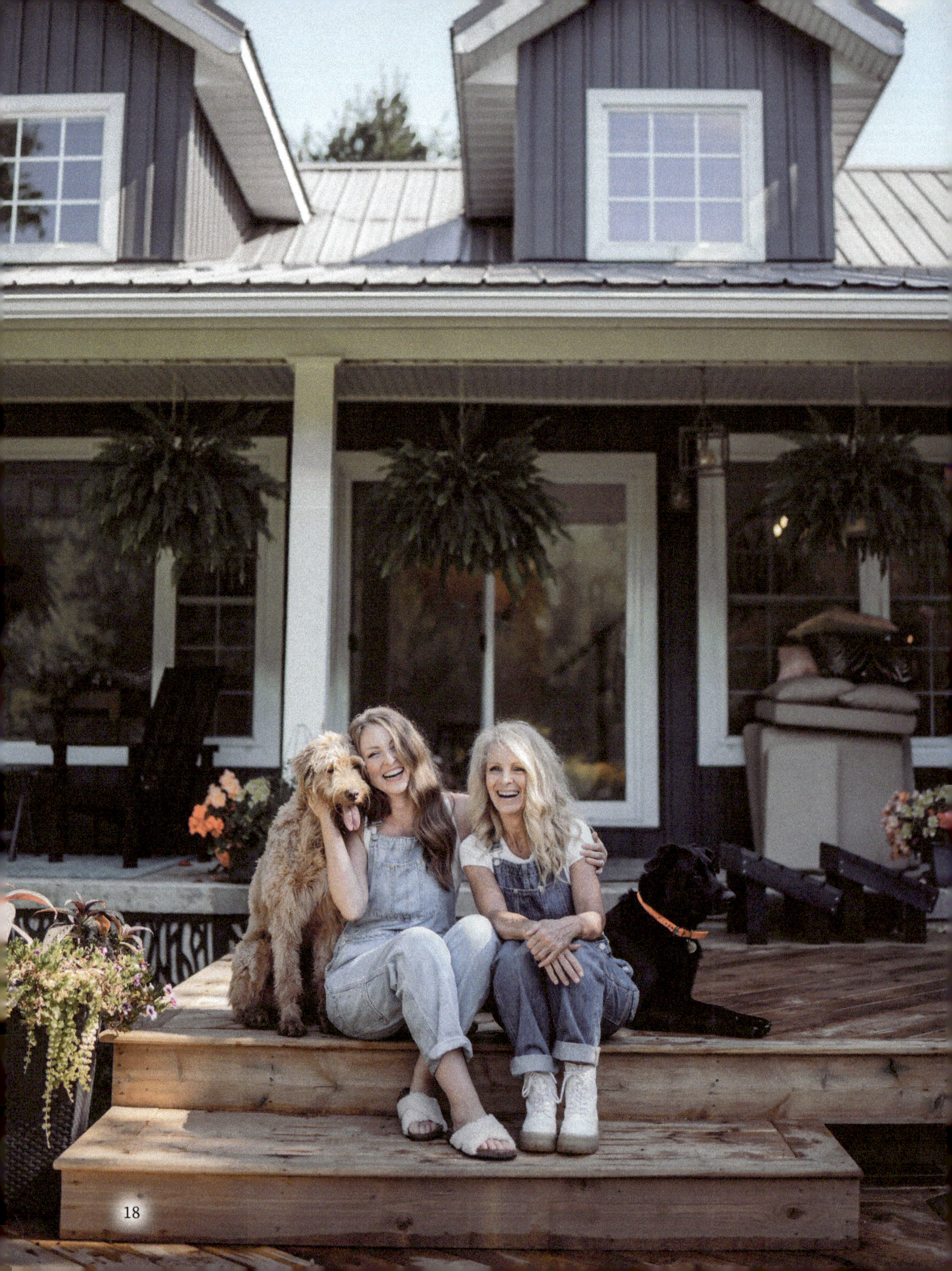

The Conscious Pantry

YOUR GATEWAY TO YOUR BEST LIFE EVER.
Over the past few decades, people's health has declined. It's hard to keep up with the chaos of misinformation, and mass media advertising drugs and junk foods. That's why we want to share with you the foods that we feel are the real body-makers. These are the ingredients we keep in our kitchen pantries 24/7, 365 days a year, and that we believe are the most vital on a plant-based diet. We don't simply buy optimal life-changing ingredients if we are feeling sickly or tired or have been diagnosed with a disease that we want to reverse. No sirree. This is a full-time gig for us. Living in poor health and eating sickly, nutrition-deprived foods is not an option.

By reading this book, you understand that your attention to your health has to come before anything else in your life. Without good health, it's virtually impossible to thrive and live a *big life*. Who doesn't want a big life?! You are here for a reason: to honor your soul's journey. It's not to play small. Plant-based foods are just part of this journey. Truly, we believe that everyone's body has different demands placed upon it at various stages of their lives. Don't be surprised when you get the intuitive call in your soul that you need to eat a certain way. Maybe at a certain stage in your life, you are getting called to do a juice or water fast. Maybe more protein is beckoning you. Maybe you feel like you need more iron or more minerals in your diet. Your body is a brilliant machine that knows best, and it is in your best interest to listen to that voice inside of you.

So, what does it mean to *eat consciously?* For us, it means eating healthy, nutrient-dense food and being aware of its source of origin and nutritional content. It is also about being aware of its flavors and textures and taking the time to be grateful and enjoy the food that nourishes us. We have spent years eating consciously and have experienced the love you cultivate with yourself when you are creating a better body and a better life.

It's about doing what's right for you. Just listen to your body, savor these delicious meals, and you'll feel amazing.

Superfoods

In this pantry section, we are putting the spotlight on the healthy superfoods we eat to thrive. These foods are ALWAYS in our kitchen to use at any time. If you want to eat better, it only makes sense to surround yourself with better food and to remove the toxic food from your kitchen cupboards and refrigerator. That way, there is no temptation to fall off the wagon.

ALMONDS

We only use raw, organic almonds. We also try to get them from Italy because California almonds are usually irradiated. According to a study done by Harvard University, "An ounce of almonds (which is about a quarter cup or twenty almonds) provides 6 grams of plant protein, 4 grams of fiber (13 percent of the daily minimum), half of the daily requirement of vitamin E, and a quarter of the daily minimum of magnesium." It also has several B vitamins, as well as calcium, potassium, and iron.

We need vitamin E as it acts as an antioxidant to protect cells from damage from disease and stress. Magnesium helps us sleep, balances our moods, and regulates our blood sugar.

Raw almonds are useful as snacks on the road and to make nut milks, chia pudding, almond butter for sandwiches, and cheesecake crusts.

APPLE CIDER VINEGAR (ACV)

Apple cider vinegar is made from apple juice that has been fermented twice. It starts with crushed apples mixed with yeast, sugar, or another carbohydrate. After a few weeks, natural bacteria and yeasts ferment the juice, changing the carbohydrates into alcohol. Then a second fermentation process changes the alcohol into acetic acid—and you have apple cider vinegar.

We buy raw apple cider vinegar for health reasons because it contains more natural yeasts and bacteria. Sometimes you may see some sediment at the bottom that appears cloudy. That is called "the mother." The mother is the fermenting starter for other batches and was used to create the vinegar in that bottle.

There are many health benefits of ACV. ACV is known to prevent acid reflux. It has also been shown to help with blood-sugar management: 2 tablespoons of diluted ACV per day can reduce blood-sugar levels.

Apple cider vinegar is known to help you lose weight. It churns up the metabolic rate and helps the body burn unwanted calories. It also helps with appetite control and fat burning in the body.

We use ACV on our hair and scalp as a final rinse. An apple cider vinegar rinse can help restore the glow of your hair, scalp, and skin. Mix one tablespoon of apple cider vinegar with two cups of water and keep in a plastic bottle in the shower. Pour on head and let sit. Then rinse briefly for about five seconds.

ASHWAGANDHA

Ashwagandha has been used as a natural stress reliever for centuries and is one of the most important adaptogenic herbs in the world. Adaptogens help the body deal with both physical and mental stress and can also reduce cortisol levels. All adaptogenic herbs help bring the body into equilibrium by regulating hormones and healing the thyroid and adrenal glands.

AVOCADO

We use avocados every day. While you might hear some people say to stay away from avocados because of the fat, avocados are full of a *healthy* fat that keeps you full and satiated. Our brains need good fat, and our bodies require fat to slow down the breakdown of carbs. This helps to keep blood-sugar levels stable.

We use avocados in our smoothies, on a salad or in a quinoa bowl, and on toast, or we eat them right out of the skin. Avocados are a great source of many vitamins. They also provide good eye and skin health with lutein, beta-carotene, and omega-3 fatty acids.

If you have excess avocados ripening too quick, cut them up and put them in a baggy in the freezer to pull out later for your smoothies!

BARLEY GRASS POWDER

Barley grass powder comes from baby barley plants. These small plants are sown and harvested, and then dried out and made into a nutritious powder. When harvested at this point of the plant's life, it is full of nutrients because it is in its super-growth stage. Barley grass is very high in certain minerals, vitamins, and antioxidants, including magnesium (vital for our human body and energy production), phosphorus (for bone-building health), and vitamins A and C (which are antioxidants that rid our bodies of free radicals). It is also comprised of complete amino acids, making it one of the most nutrient-dense foods in the world.

We add barley grass powder to our green smoothies to increase our optimal nutrition intake. It can also be added to dips and even salad dressings to make a salad into a "superfood" salad!

BASIL

Basil is a multi-purpose herb that you can easily grow in your backyard, balcony, or even in your kitchen. Add it to all salads and most meals. Basil isn't simply for eating. Due to its antibacterial properties, basil oil is wonderful for treating cuts, wounds, and skin infections, according to the NIH.

If you have a lot of fresh basil, you can dry the leaves and store them in a jar with a tight-fitting lid. Avoid crumbling the leaves until you need them, as this helps retain their essential oils, aroma, and flavor.

BEE POLLEN

Feeling like your allergies are kicking in? Try bee pollen. It is known to boost the immune system of allergy sufferers. Bee pollen contains a wide variety of antioxidants, which can protect your cells from damage caused by free radicals that are linked to chronic diseases, including cancer and type-2 diabetes.

Bee pollen is a mixture of flower pollen, honey, nectar, enzymes, wax, and bee secretions. It may sound kind of weird, but it is powerfully healthy for you. A Russian study of the people of Georgia (where many live to be over one hundred years old) revealed that many of these centenarians were beekeepers who often ate raw, unprocessed honey with all of its unfiltered impurities (i.e., bee pollen).

Remarkably, bee pollen contains twenty-two amino acids, including all eight essential ones. It also contains twenty-seven minerals, and much-needed vitamins, fatty acids, and even hormones. These are the BUILDING BLOCKS of life.

Bee pollen can be taken in capsule form or powder. We use it in smoothies and sometimes sprinkle it on top of jam on some whole-grain toast.

CACAO/CACAO NIBS

Cacao is the #1 source of magnesium of any food on the earth. It also contains the highest concentration of antioxidants of any food in the world.

Wait! There's more! It also has the highest source of iron of any plant and is exceptionally rich in zinc, copper, EFA, serotonin, chromium, anandamide (the bliss chemical), and more.

We love cacao for how it makes us feel. Imagine savoring a piece of 90% dark chocolate and letting it melt in your mouth. OOOOooooooooooh. Or how about when you make yourself a cup of oat-milk hot chocolate, sip on it, and feel your mood lifting? Cacao (raw cocoa) has theobromine in it, which when ingested gives us the similar feeling of being in love. Why do we run to chocolate to soothe us from break-ups or sadness? We intuitively know it gives us the warm comfort that we need in that moment.

Cacao nibs are chunky little pieces of the cacao bean pod and are delicious in smoothies, granola, chia puddings, and cookies.

CHIA SEEDS

Chia seeds are an ancient Aztec and Mayan superfood. The word "chia" means strength in the Mayan language. This concentrated protein seed is rich in fiber, which helps keep the body full and energized for hours. The amount of calcium found in chia seeds is considered to be higher than what is found in skimmed milk. (Who needs cow's milk?) These seeds also contain boron, phosphorus, and zinc, which help to work with calcium to increase bone and teeth health.

Chia seeds can be used to make chia puddings (like we do every two to three days and store in our refrigerator), be added to baked goods, or sprinkled on cereal or savory dishes. We make "chia eggs" for baking by adding 3 tablespoons of water to 1 tablespoon of chia seeds. They expand into a gel, which makes them a great, plant-based egg-replacement option.

CILANTRO

This is a powerhouse heavy-metal detox. We have used cilantro for over a decade to eradicate heavy metals from our bodies. Heavy metals build up from a toxic life using toxic chemicals to clean with, fluoridated drinking water, fast foods, and even pollution from the air we breathe. We add cilantro to green smoothies, salads, chia puddings (for real!), taco toppers, soup garnishes, and anywhere we can get away with it.

COCONUT BUTTER

Have you ever spread coconut butter on toast and then topped it with avocado and sea salt? Delicious!

With its antibacterial properties, coconut butter helps to prevent disease. It also boosts immunity. In fact, research has shown that next to a mother's milk for a newborn, coconut is the second-best way to strengthen the immune system. And did you know that coconut butter contains fiber? It's actually a high-fiber food that works to help control blood sugar levels. We use coconut butter on our hair because it helps to keep it shiny and healthy. It is easily absorbed and moisturizes the hair to prevent dandruff and brittle dryness. We also use it like a leave in conditioner once a month to keep our locks looking great!

Try stirring coconut butter into your coffee, hot chocolate, or lattes to make them creamy. Or add coconut butter to smoothies or oatmeal or porridge for a healthier breakfast. You can also use it to make raw fudge or other raw, plant-based treats. Coconut butter is rich and healthy.

COCONUT MILK

When we talk about coconut milk, we are speaking of canned coconut milk that is white, creamy, and thick. It should not be confused with coconut water, which is found naturally in immature green coconuts. Unlike coconut water, we have to make coconut milk from scratch or buy it canned because it is not created naturally. Rather solid coconut flesh is blended on high speed with water to make coconut milk.

If there is a healthy food that you want to incorporate into your life more often, it's coconut milk. It also happens to be truly rich and delicious. There are so many places to use it in the kitchen like chia puddings, smoothies, lattes, sauces, and dressings. We have at least six to ten cans in our pantry to use in a moment's notice.

Coconut milk is dense with lauric acid, which is known to protect your health. Lauric acid is easily absorbed and used by the body.

COCONUT OIL

Coconut oil has been a primary fat for tropical diets for quite literally centuries. Coconut oil is high in certain saturated fats called medium chain fatty acids. These particular fats have a very unique effect on the body compared to other fats, as they go straight to your liver and are metabolized there. Your body is then able to use them as a quick source of energy unlike other fats.

Coconut oil also has many medicinal and health benefits. Coconut oil contains lauric acid (also found in breast milk), which is antibacterial and antiviral. When we get a scrape or a cut, we put coconut oil on it to help with the healing of it. We also use coconut oil as a mouthwash. Swirl it around to "oil pull" bacteria out of your mouth and to help keep your gums pink and healthy.

According to Dr. Axe, "coconut oil has antibacterial properties so it can reduce candida, fight bacteria, and create a hostile environment for viruses." Almost half of the fat in coconut is lauric acid, which helps destroy active bacteria in the gut.

We use coconut oil to sauté kale in our iron skillets with a little sea salt. Coconut oil can be used for everything that you would use any other oil for in your kitchen. We also use it on our legs to keep them smooth and moisturized.

Side Note on Fats: When we talk about fats in this book, we're talking about all of the incredible healthy, plant-based fats that fuel your cells and your body and keep you vibrant and strong! All fats are not created equal, but they are vital for keeping your brain healthy.

GINGER PAGE 25

FLAXSEED

Remarkably, humans have been consuming flaxseed for over six thousand years. Flax can be used as an egg substitute for plant-based baking. They are known for their high levels of heart-healthy omega-3, an essential fatty acid required by the body. Each tablespoon of flaxseeds contains about 1.8 grams of plant-based omega-3s.

Flaxseeds are tiny, brown- or golden-colored seeds, which are also known as linseed. They are more beneficial and more bio-available to humans when sprouted or ground into flax meal. (We grind our own in a coffee-bean grinder and then put the flax meal in a baggy and store it in the freezer).

GINGER

Ginger can be used fresh, dried, powdered, or as an oil or juice. It has many health benefits from being an anti-nausea that will calm a stressed belly (women with morning sickness respond well to ginger) to having immune building properties. Fresh ginger is rich with antioxidant and anti-inflammatory properties. It's great to have on hand to make a ginger tea for cold and flu season.

HEMP SEEDS

Hemp seeds have superfood qualities unlike any other food out there. They are rich in healthy fats, improve skin, joints and heart health.

Hemp seeds have been given a bad rap due to being associated with the cannabis plant, and it is funny that the hallucinogen side, THC, is hitting the mainstream with stores on every corner now, but it is still hard to find hemp flour on the shelves. Sometimes we really wonder if the government and big corporations are on our side. If they were, hemp would be mandated in every home.

These seeds are a complete source of protein, meaning that they provide all nine essential amino acids. Amino acids are the building blocks for all proteins. The body cannot produce these nine amino acids, so a person must absorb them through their diet. Relatively few plant-based foods are complete sources of protein, making hemp seeds a valuable addition to a vegetarian or vegan diet. Hemp seeds contain almost as much protein as soybeans. In every 30 grams of seeds (about 3 tablespoons) there are 10 grams of protein.

Hemp seeds are a powerhouse of nutrition. Imagine all of this healthy "potential" being bundled up in a little seed ready to explode into a thriving plant—and we get to eat it.

KELP NOODLES

We like kelp noodles because they are so easy to use. You simply toss them into a salad and enjoy. They are also low in calories and naturally gluten-free. Made from a brown seaweed that grows in deep waters, kelp noodles can be purchased in Asian grocery stores and some health-food stores.

LEMON (ALKALINE FOR THE BODY)

Lemons are a staple in our kitchens! They are high in vitamin C, they are alkalizing to the body and have been known to treat various health ailments.

We drink a full twelve- to sixteen-ounce glass of lemon water every morning before anything else. We know it promotes hydration in our cells and supports a good weight-management program. The cleansing effect of lemon water will make your skin look better and aid digestion to help keep your stomach flat and toned.

LEMON BALM

The most beneficial natural health remedies are often the ones that have been around the longest, and the use of lemon balm has been around for centuries. In modern times, it has been studied for its effects on insomnia all the way to cancer. It is a powerful antioxidant and is known for protection against anxiety, brain fog, or a nervous stomachache. You'll be both calmed and energized by its citrus-minty flavor. It soothes the body from irritations to give you mental clarity. Lemon balm also improves skin appearance. The great thing about lemon balm is that you can feel the effects immediately, and it also has long-term benefits as well!

Over the past two years, we have started to grow it in our garden. It grows fast, just like its cousin the mint plant. You never have to worry about overharvesting, and because it is a perennial, it will come up again every spring. No need to start over with new seeds or seedlings.

Lemon balm can be found in most healthy grocery stores and can be brewed up daily or specifically if you are under stress. You can even steep a few teabags in a large pot of water and let it chill in the refrigerator for iced tea. Lemon balm can be pureed with other fruits (like peaches) to make popsicles. We make tea, which is good hot or cold, to help us sleep at night and it really takes the edge off anxious moments throughout the day.

MACA

Maca is a thyroid-supporting food with 18 amino acids. It increases energy levels and helps to boost your mood and balance hormones. It works really well with anxiety and helps us adapt to stressors. We use it in powder form and add it to smoothies and lattes and stir it into oatmeal.

MANUKA HONEY

Manuka honey is a superfood. Harvested from the unique Manuka tree in New Zealand, it has very unusual properties compared to any other honey. Although all honey contains antimicrobial properties, only Manuka honey contains non-hydrogen peroxide, which gives it a greater antibacterial power.

Manuka honey is a great source of zinc, sodium, potassium, phosphorus, manganese, magnesium, iron, copper, calcium, B vitamins, and amino acids. Manuka honey, like other raw honeys, is good for first aid and treating burns or wounds due to its powerful antibacterial quality.

> DYK: Honey has been known to improve cognitive function and reduce anxiety!

MATCHA MORNING LATTES
(We like the Harmonic Arts brand.)

Matcha comes from the *Camellia sinensis* plant—just like green tea. However, it is grown differently, which changes its nutrient profile. Matcha is grown by farmers covering their green tea plants for twenty to thirty days before harvest to avoid the sun hitting the plants directly. Incredibly, this increases chlorophyll production. It also gives the tea a darker green color and boosts the tea's amino acid content.

Matcha is rich in antioxidants that help to stabilize harmful free radicals. It also potentially offers protection against cancers and other diseases.

We drink a matcha latte almost every day. Sometimes we mix it up a bit and make the lattes with oat milk or almond or cashew milk (or a half and half). Be creative! We also add lion's mane, reishi, or chaga mushroom extract to our lattes as well to make superfood lattes!

MEDICINAL MUSHROOMS: chaga, cordyceps, lion's mane, and reishi

The use of medicinal mushrooms for health reasons dates back centuries. Due to their very unique and truly varied adaptive benefits for health, we are seeing a resurgence of people choosing to take control of their health, live more naturally, and eat these fabulous superfoods. We believe medicinal mushrooms can push our health up a few more notches when we incorporate them into our life. The good news is that it is very easy to use them every day. They all come in tinctures, powder form, or in capsules so you can choose how you want to incorporate them.

Chaga mushrooms boost digestion and clears/protects skin. They are rich in antioxidants and support immune function, liver health, and brain health, and increase longevity. We put chaga mushroom powder in our smoothies every day. It can also be easily incorporated in porridge, gluten-free baking, salad dressings, ice cream, and lattes.

Cordyceps mushrooms improve lung capacity and increase energy, so they are sometimes used to treat lung-related issues like asthma or even seasonal allergies.

Lion's mane mushrooms support healthy brain function and neuron regeneration. They are even shaped like a brain! When we saw one for the first time at a farmers' market, we took it home and made a mushroom side dish with it. We didn't know what we were doing, but it was delicious!

Reishi mushrooms work as a sleep aid and potent immuno-modulator. If taken over time, they can significantly support the immune system. They also improve sleep and reduce stress and fatigue. You can find them in dropper form in many health-food stores. We take a full dropper in our water throughout the day, especially when stressed out.

OATS

Look for certified gluten-free and organic oats. We use Bob's Red Mill brand. Oats are good for fiber and delicious in cookies. Have you tried overnight oats? They are an easy way to create a nutritious breakfast the night before. In a small mason jar, simply add 2 cups of your choice of plant-based milk and 1 cup of oats, and a splash of maple syrup. Give it a good shake and leave it in the fridge overnight. When you wake up, you'll have the perfect breakfast!

QUINOA

Quinoa is so easy to use and implement in your diet. For the busy household, you can make a big pot of it every few days and store it in the refrigerator to pull from to make "on the fly" meals. Quinoa is nutrient rich, a good source of protein, and has many health benefits. This grain/seed was considered sacred by the Incas. Quinoa can help you create a healthier version of you.

SPIRULINA

Spirulina is a blue-green algae known for its powerful health benefits. The quality of the protein in spirulina is ideal, bar none; it is one of the most complete proteins available to us. It provides all the essential amino acids that you need. Gram for gram, spirulina may be the single most nutritious food on the planet. A tablespoon (approximately 7 grams) of spirulina provides a very small amount of fat (about 1 gram), and this includes both omega-6 and omega-3 (in a perfectly natural healthy ratio of 1.5–1.0).

We add spirulina to pretty much all of our green smoothies. This way we know we are getting as much optimal nutrition into our bodies as possible. We store ours in the fridge to ensure it stays as fresh as possible. It can be found at most grocery stores in the natural foods section or health-food stores.

SUNFLOWER SEEDS (AND BUTTER)

Sunflower seeds are harvested from the large flower heads of the sunflower. Sunflower seeds are great for fueling bone health. Many people believe calcium is what protects their bones, but that is merely one of a group or team of minerals responsible for optimal bone health. Sunflower seeds are made up of bone-health minerals like magnesium, phosphorus, and copper. They are also great for immune health with their high amounts of zinc and selenium. Enjoy sunflower seeds in their seed form or as sunflower-seed butter, a great alternative to peanut butter!

> DYK: "A sunflower can measure more than twelve inches (30.5 cm) in diameter, and a single sunflower head may contain up to two thousand seeds"—According to Healthline

TAHINI

Tahini is a paste (like peanut butter) made from toasted and ground sesame seeds. It has a light, nutty flavor. Sesame seeds contain a high content of methionine and tryptophan, two amino acids usually lacking in vegetable foods.

It's best known as an important ingredient in hummus, but it works well as a peanut substitute in virtually any recipe that calls for peanut butter. The high vitamin E and antioxidants content make it resistant to rancidity, and therefore it can extend the shelf life of hummus and other dishes. Tahini can be spread on toast, used as a veggie dip, or swirled into a soup.

TURMERIC (CURCUMIN)

Fresh turmeric is found as an actual root in the grocery store. It is also found in the spice section in powder form. We have used turmeric many times for its yellow food coloring. You only need a little. It's great to use when we want to make yellow frosting like for our lemon or pina colada cupcakes.

This spice powerhouse is an incredible antioxidant that can provide protection for your health and healing for your body. We use it in curries and some sauces. We also take curcumin capsules every day for hormone regulation and to protect our bodies from inflammation.

If we buy it in the fresh root form, we juice it (use about one inch) with ginger root (about one inch), lemon, apples, and oranges to make a tonic that keeps colds and flus away.

WHITE PINE NEEDLE TINCTURE

White pine needles are rich in vitamin C (five times the concentration of vitamin C found in lemons) and can bring relief to conditions such as heart disease, varicose veins, skin issues, and feelings of exhaustion. Vitamin C is also an immune-system booster, which means that pine needle tincture can help to fight illness and infections.

Pine needle tincture also contains high levels of vitamin A, which is good for your eyesight, improves hair and skin regeneration, and increases red blood cell production. It can be used as an expectorant for coughs and to help relieve chest congestion; it is also good for sore throats.

Mentally speaking, pine needle tincture brings you mental clearness. It can also help with depression, obesity, allergies, and high blood pressure.

Pine needles contain antioxidants. These reduce free radicals, which are harmful to humans and can cause disease. White pine needles also contain shikimic acid. This is antiviral and used in many anti-flu and anti-virus preparations. Other sources of shikimate are fennel (star anise) tea and schizandra tea.

WILD BLUEBERRIES

Wild blueberries are a powerhouse of antioxidants. They have two times the antioxidants of conventional blueberries. Even the taste of wild blueberries is different; they have a stronger and tangier taste than the cultivated kind. Blueberry smoothies, blueberry sundaes, blueberries on salads, and blueberry muffins mean we keep about four one-pound bags in the freezer at all times. We love them too because they are about eighty calories per cup.

DIGESTIVE TINCTURE
PAGE 56/57

THE CONSCIOUS PANTRY

TURMERIC PAGE 28

Conscious Grocery Shopping

Seeing where your food comes from and knowing it is farmed in a way that protects the planet and brings a fair wage to the farmers, brings an extra level of consciousness and gratitude for the food on your plate. So, we do our best to *always* buy organic and fair-trade foods, and we strive to buy local when possible. We love going to local farmers markets and produce stands and buying the imperfect veggies and fruit—as that picture-perfect produce you always hunt for is usually covered in preservatives, wax, and chemicals. And, of course, we always bring our own reusable bags when shopping. When we forget, we ask for a box to put everything in instead of using plastic bags.

We also shop in the natural-food section of our grocery store for our pantry items and the perimeter of the store for some of our organic produce. Why just the perimeter?! Because the inside aisles are usually full of corn, soy, sugar, and unhealthy preservative-filled, pre-packaged foods.

GROCERY LIST

In this section, you'll find the most up-to-date list of the pantry essentials that are usually in our cupboards, fridge, and freezer along with the superfoods mentioned in the last section. We keep it very brief and to the point to make your grocery shopping quick and painless. You'll need many of these ingredients to prepare the recipes in this cookbook. Most of these ingredients can be found in grocery stores and natural-food stores, or for a few less popular ingredients, with a quick search online.

In the Cupboard

Legumes: We use canned legumes (canned is so much easier!) as an extra dose of protein in soups, salads, and dips.

- Black beans
- Chickpeas
- Kidney beans
- Lentils (keep a variety)

Nuts and Seeds: Packed with nutrients, nuts and seeds are great in your morning cereal; in batters and dough when baking; to enjoy as a snack; and to turn into plant-based milks. If you have an abundant supply of nuts and seeds in your pantry, it is best to store them in the freezer to keep them fresher longer.

- Almonds
- Cashews
- Chia seeds
- Flaxseeds
- Hemp seeds
- Pine nuts
- Pumpkin seeds
- Sunflower seeds
- Walnuts

Whole Grains: These reap the most health benefits and fuel your body; be sure to add a variety to your diet.

- Brown rice
- Buckwheat
- Millet
- Quinoa which is actually a seed
- Rolled oats

Pastas: Use healthier alternatives to traditional pasta. And when making pasta, be sure to add some extra veggies! Pasta makes for a super easy dinner!

- Brown rice pasta
- Kelp noodles
- Mung bean pasta
- Quinoa pasta
- Sweet potato pasta

Oils, Fats and Vinegars: Use in place of animal-based oils for salads and cooking.

- Apple cider vinegar
- Avocado oil
- Organic Fair-Trade Palm Shortening
  (We use "Palm Done Right")
- Balsamic vinegar
- Coconut oil

THE CONSCIOUS PANTRY | 31

- Extra-virgin olive oil
- Grapeseed oil
- Red wine vinegar
- Vegan butter (Earth balance is great!)

Condiments: Add them to your favorite dishes for a boost of flavor!

- Miso paste
- Organic hot sauce
- Sriracha sauce
- Tahini
- Wheat-free tamari

Dry Goods: These are essential for the recipes throughout this book, from breakfast to dessert; they are so good for you and add so much flavor!

- Blue corn tortillas chips
- Coconut shreds
- Corn grits
- Dried blueberries (these are quite expensive!)
- Dried mushrooms
- Nori sheets
- Nutritional yeast
- Wakame

Canned and Jarred Goods: These can be a tasty addition to any meal, and you never know when you'll need them! Make sure they are gluten-free, low sodium, and organic.

- Baked beans
- Coconut milk, full fat
- Diced tomatoes
- Jackfruit
- Lemon/lime juice
- Pumpkin puree
- Sundried tomatoes
- Tahini

Organic Dried Herbs and Spices: Buy ground or whole (as specified) and in bulk at your local health-food store.

- Basil
- Black pepper
- Cayenne
- Chili flakes
- Cinnamon
- Cumin Buy ground and whole!
- Curry
- Garlic powder
- Himalayan sea salt
- Onion powder
- Rosemary
- Sage
- Thyme

Baking: Plant-based and gluten-free baking is SO easy!

- Arrowroot starch
- Almond flour
- Baking powder
- Baking soda
- Coconut flour
- Gluten-free all-purpose flour We love Bob's Red Mill!
- Potato starch
- Quinoa flour

> **Egg Replacements**
> We use whole flaxseeds, ground flaxseeds, or chia seeds. Just use one tablespoon of seeds with three tablespoons of water, let sit for about five minutes, and voila, you have an egg!

Sweeteners: We use sweeteners in various ways from morning to evening. Lower glycemic sweeteners like dates and monk fruit powder are great in the morning to keep your insulin levels lower, and more conventional sweeteners like cane sugar and Sucanat are great in baked goods.

- Brown rice syrup
- Coconut sugar
- Date sugar
- Maple syrup
- Medjool dates
- Molasses
- Monk fruit powder
- Organic fair-trade sugar
- Raw Manuka honey (also a superfood)

- Stevia powder
- Sucanat A raw form of sugar

In the Fridge

Kombucha: This is a fermented, naturally effervescent tea. Kombucha is an incredible digestive aid and helps to keep your gut health optimal. It's a staple in our fridges. Keep it refrigerated, and don't shake it unless you want a kombucha explosion! Consider yourself warned. :)

Plant-Based Milks: It's always nice to make your milks at home (pages 51–53). But if you're tight on time, you can always use store-bought—no pressure. Just try to find options with as little additives and preservatives as possible. These are found in the refrigerated section of your grocery store or in tetra packs on the shelf of your local grocery store. We like to have a variety of sweetened and unsweetened options in our pantry.

- Almond milk
- Cashew milk
- Coconut milk
- Oat milk
- Soy milk

Nut Butters & Alternatives: Can be found in the natural food section of your grocery store.

- Almond butter
- Cacao butter
- Cashew butter
- Coconut butter
- Peanut Butter Organic is best.
- Sunflower seed butter

Other Plant-Based Alternatives:

- Tempeh Fermented soybean patty
- Tofu
- Vegan cheese
- Vegan mayo
- Vegan shortening
- Vegan yogurt

Vegetables: We always like to have a good selection of seasonal veggies in our kitchen.

- Carrots
- Celery
- Dark leafy greens (kale, spinach, collard greens, Swiss chard)
- Mushrooms (cremini, portabella, enoki, oyster, shitake)
- Onions (Spanish and red onion)
- Peppers (red, green, orange peppers, and jalapeno peppers for some spice!)

Fruits: We like to chop and portion out our fruit to ensure it gets eaten! Cut fruits make for such a great snack! We love to freeze local berries when they are in season to be used in the off-season. Don't forget frozen bananas are the bomb for smoothies.

- Apples
- Bananas
- Berries (Strawberries, raspberries, wild blueberries, blackberries)
- Lemons
- Mango
- Papaya
- Pineapple
- Pink dragon fruit

Fresh Herbs and Roots: Freshens up any meal! We always peel (the roots) and chop!

- Basil
- Cilantro
- Ginger Root
- Oregano
- Rosemary
- Sage
- Thyme (Did you know juiced thyme can kill cold-sore viruses?)
- Turmeric Root

In the Freezer

- Chopped frozen bananas Great for smoothies!
- Plant-based ice cream We love Coconut Bliss Ice Cream!
- Skinny Cookies from Kelly's Bake Shoppe
- Wild blueberries, organic raspberries, organic strawberries

MILKS PAGE 50-53

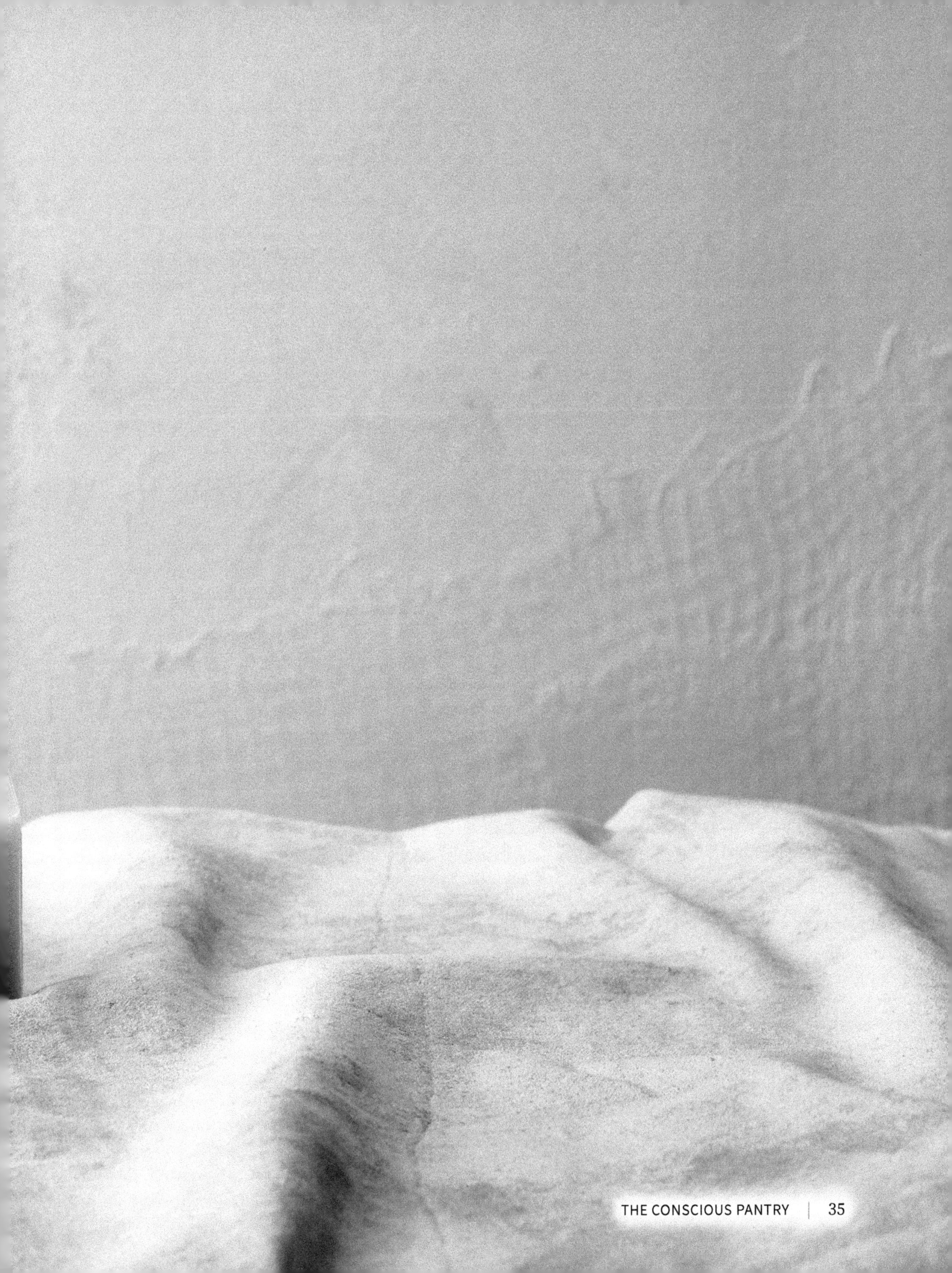

Kitchen Tools

Here's a list of some essentials that we love to have in our kitchens. Of course, there are so many we could list, but these are our favorites. Be sure to have these tools on hand!

- **Cast-iron skillet:** These are fantastic for so many reasons. We season ours by rubbing olive oil into the pan with a paper towel and then sprinkling it with sea salt. They cook evenly, are chemical-free, and have an incredibly long lifespan!

- **Chef's knife and paring knife:** Ahhhh, the value of a good, sharp knife! It makes prep so much easier (and much safer than a dull knife), especially if you're chopping lots of veggies (which you will for our recipes). Invest in a knife sharpener too!

- **Electric hand mixer or stand mixer:** An essential all around. A hand mixer is great for quick and easy baking, and for mashing potatoes, and makes for a quick clean-up. If you're wanting to take it up a notch, we suggest investing in a countertop stand mixer. The average home mixer is 2.2 quarts. We use a 60-quart mixer at the bake shoppe.

- **Food processor:** We have a 14-cup food processor. It is great for dips like hummus, spreads, and even raw vegan cookie dough. We also have a smaller one to puree sunflower seeds to make nut butter and to make small batches of our "Nut Parmesan, page 198" and pestos.

- **Glass jars for canning:** Admittedly, we don't do a ton of canning—maybe twice in our life. We do, however, use canning jars (large and small) for the juices and smoothies we make every day. Canning jars can also be used for chia puddings. Just shake the pudding base with the chia seeds and place in the refrigerator to thicken.

- **Heavy-duty blender:** This is for smoothies, sauces, and soups. It's such a great investment, and we use one every day. Our brand of choice is the top-of-the-line Vitamix 5200 and Blendtec. For making everything from velvety smoothies to soups to nut milks, it is an important tool in our kitchens.

- **Ice cream scoop—spring loaded:** This is one of our favorite go-tos at the bake shoppe. We use ice cream scoops for cookies and cupcakes and scooping the perfect amount of basically anything for our recipes.

- **Juicer:** How else are you going to experience the magic of celery juice? We own a Breville juicer, and it is used four to five times a week. Investing in your health is priceless.

- **Large-rimmed baking sheet(s):** We have hundreds of baking sheets at the bake shoppe for baking cookies, roasting bananas, letting sauces cool evenly, and so much more. We suggest a large-rimmed baking sheet because it'll help prevent any spills or burns coming out of the oven.

- **Reusable nut milk bag:** This is necessary for making almond milk and straining your milk.

- **Spiralizer:** Great for spiralizing veggies for "raw" pasta recipes.

THE CONSCIOUS PANTRY | 37

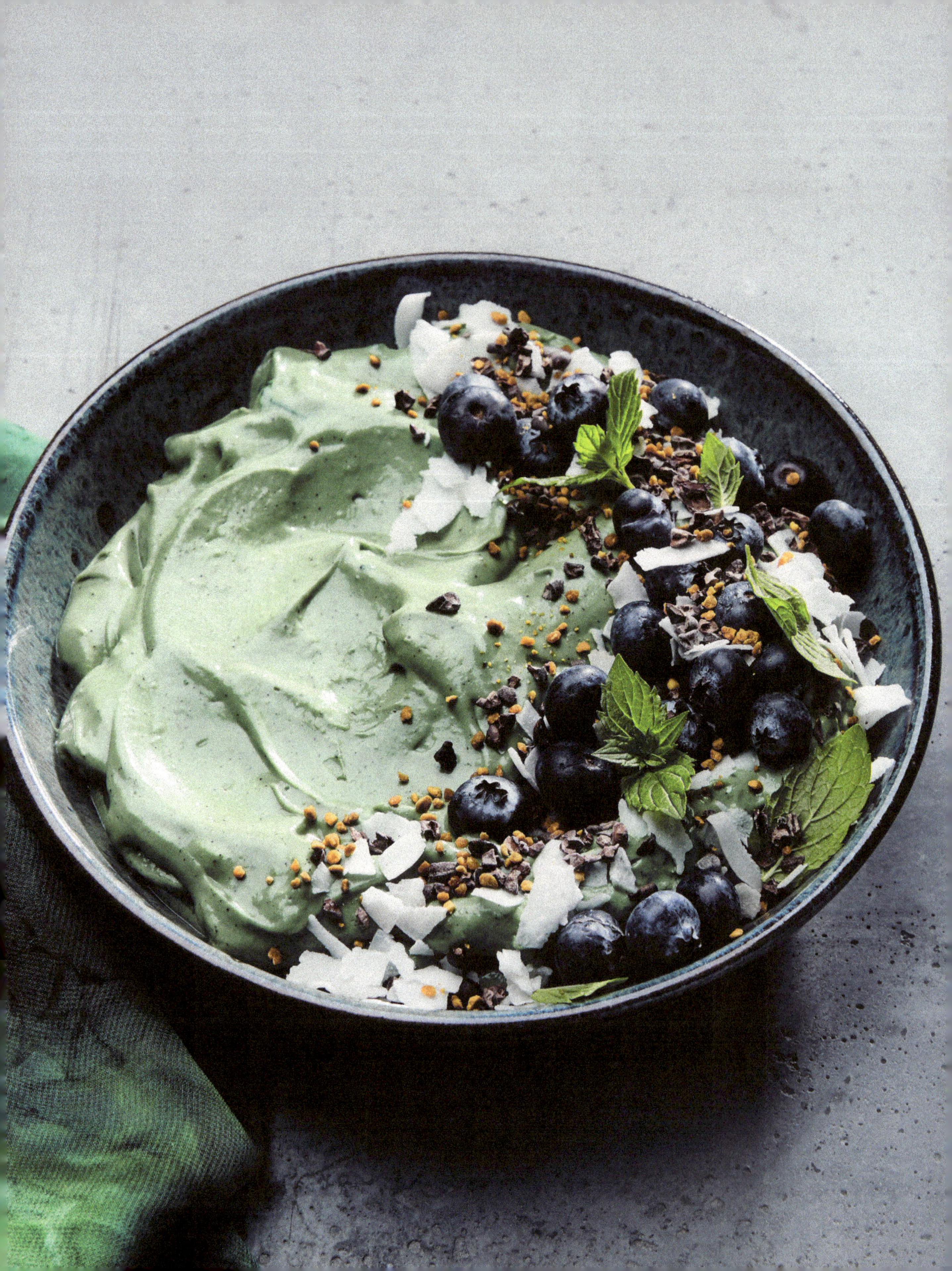

PART II

recipes for eating consciously

GRAPEFRUIT — high in vitamin C and can help to improve heart health.

Immunity Boosters

Here's some of our favourite ways to keep our immune systems healthy and vibrant, especially during cold & flu season.

DARK CHOCOLATE/CACAO — great for heart health, gut health, and happens to be delicious too.

GINGER — strong antioxidant and anti-inflammatory benefits.

TURMERIC —

Curcumin, a compound found in turmeric is known to have anti-inflammatory properties that help boost immunity.

MATCHA — high in antioxidants, great swap-out for coffee during cold and flu season.

GARLIC — helps to fight infections and viruses.

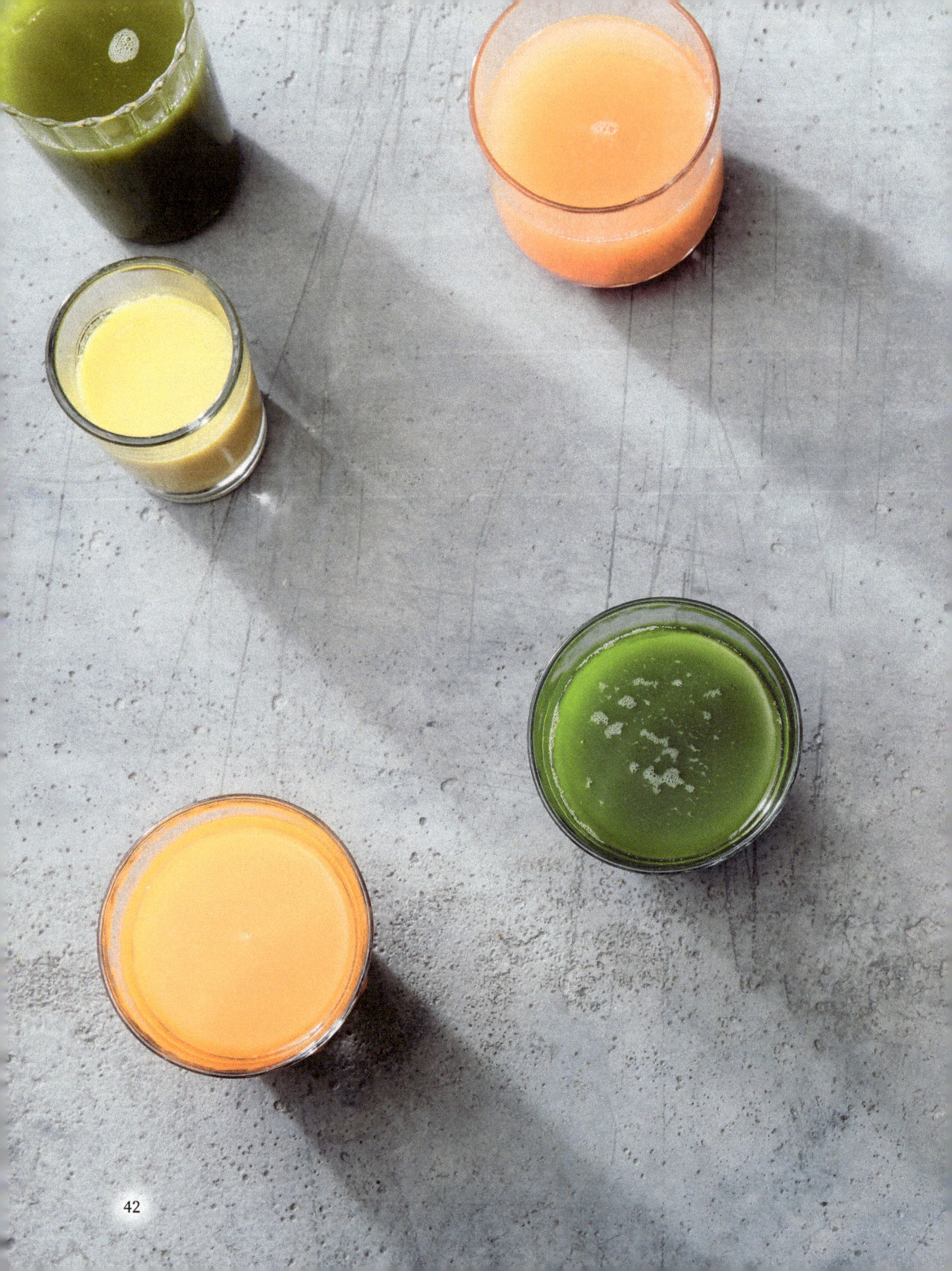

Beverages

Kelly & Erinn's Morning Matcha   44

Wake-Up Tonic   47

Supernatural Cacao "Coffee"   48

Oat Milk   51

Coconut Milk   52

Cashew Milk   53

Detox Juice   54

Digestive Tincture   57

Black Lemonade   59

Chia Agua Fresca   60

Simple Green   63

Celery Juice   64

Soul-Soothing Turmeric Tonic   67

Wellness Shot   68

White Pine Needle Tea   71

Kelly + Erinn's Morning Matcha

This is part of our daily routine. We wholeheartedly believe in the health benefits of matcha, and it's an absolute must for us to start our day off on the right foot. Matcha helps to speed up your metabolism and burn fat, and also helps to strengthen your immune system with its super high level of antioxidants. It contains a special caffeine that is more of a slow trickle in your body and is easy to adapt to (rather than the typical jolt of caffeine from coffee).

PREP TIME: 5 minutes
MAKES: 1 serving

2 cups coconut milk (page 52) or oat milk (page 51)
1 ½ tsp ceremonial grade matcha powder
1 Tbsp coconut butter
½ tsp maple syrup or raw honey
¼ tsp ashwagandha powder (see DYK)

1. In a small saucepan, bring the milk to a simmer. Set aside to cool slightly for 3 to 5 minutes. Add to blender.

2. Add the matcha powder, coconut butter, maple syrup, and ashwagandha powder to the warm milk in a blender. Blend until smooth.

3. Pour into a mug and enjoy!

TO SERVE: Taste and adjust flavor where needed. If you feel it is too bitter, add a touch more maple syrup.

DYK: Ceremonial grade matcha is made from the youngest tea leaves with all the stems and veins removed to obtain a very yummy, smooth flavor and texture.

DYK: Ashwagandha, one of the most powerful herbs in Ayurvedic healing, has been used since ancient times for a wide variety of conditions. It is most well-known for its hormonal restorative benefits and immune-boosting properties. It is available at your local health-food store.

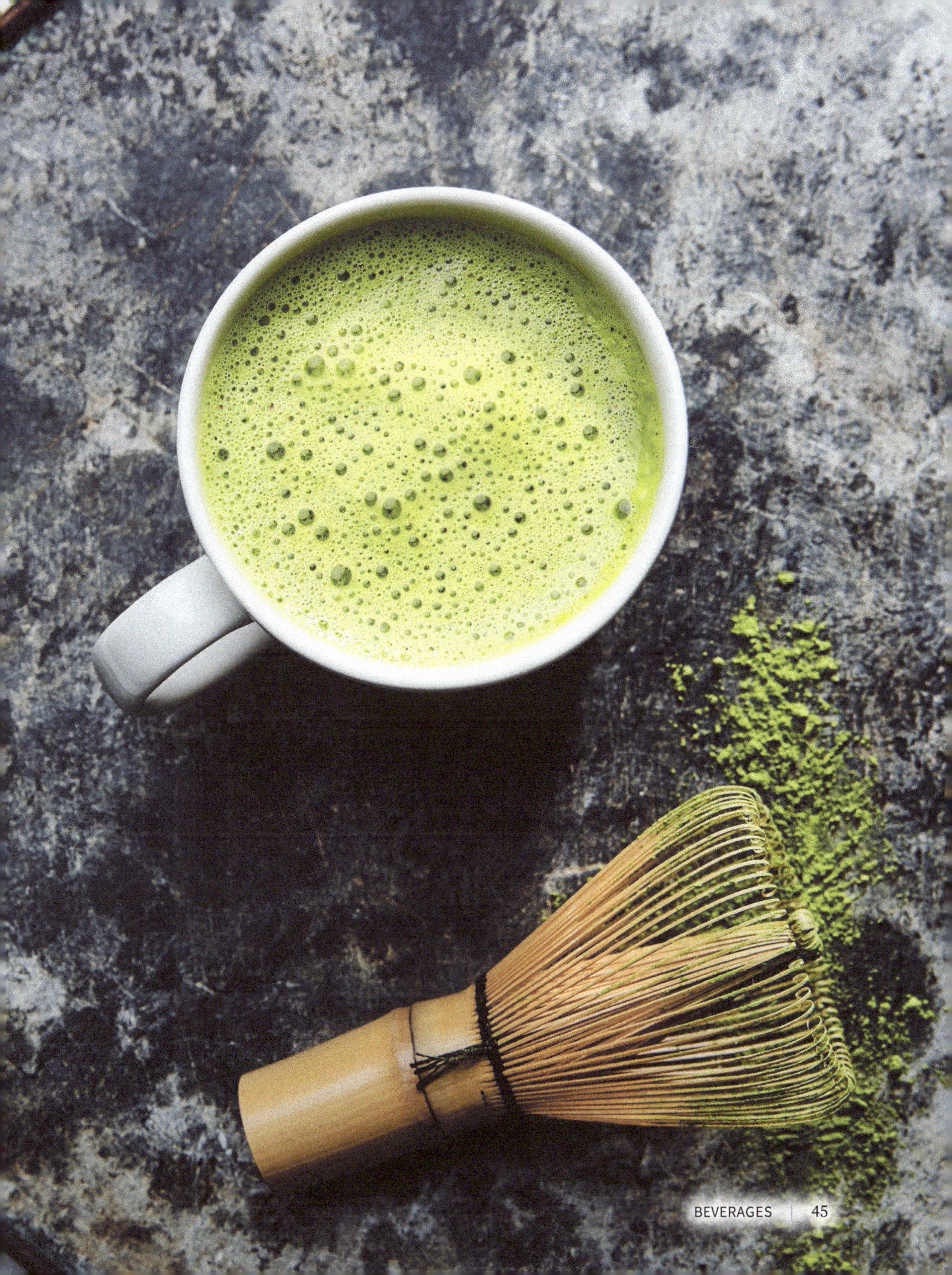

DYK: Cordyceps mushrooms have been traditionally used to increase energy levels. They can be taken in dropper or capsule form.

DYK: Lion's mane is a form of mushroom. It has been known to help with overall brain functions and cognitive health. It has also been know to help treat anxiety and depression.

Wake-Up Tonic

When you wake up, you are breaking your ten-twelve hour fast from dinnertime, and your body needs time to transition to being awake and ready for the day. Your body has worked all night, healing and detoxing itself while you slept, and the best thing you can do is to support it with a nourishing juice. Try a cleansing, healing tonic like this one:

PREP TIME: 5 minutes
MAKES: 1 serving
SHELF LIFE: 1 day

2 pink grapefruits, peeled and cut into sections

1 Tbsp turmeric root or ground turmeric

1 lemon, peeled

¼ cup pineapple, sliced

5 drops of cordyceps mushroom elixir (see DYK)

5 drops of lion's mane mushroom elixir (see DYK)

1. In the order they are listed, add the grapefruit, turmeric, lemon, and pineapple to a juicer.

2. Add the cordyceps and lion's mane to the juice container.

TO SERVE: Enjoy in a tall glass or refrigerate for the next day.

NOTE: Make sure you use the pink grapefruit variety in this recipe as it will yield the best-tasting tonic.

Supernatural Cacao "Coffee"

Bulletproof™ coffee is so popular right now thanks to the one and only, Dave Asprey! In our version, we use coconut oil and hemp seeds to make it rich and creamy, and guess what? There's no coffee or dairy! Trust us; it's the perfect addition to your morning routine.

PREP TIME: 3 minutes
MAKES: 1–2 servings

1 Tbsp raw cacao powder
2 Tbsp hemp seeds
1 Tbsp coconut oil or MCT oil
1 Tbsp raw Manuka honey or maple syrup
½ tsp chicory root powder
½ tsp reishi mushroom extract
Big pinch of cinnamon
Pinch of cayenne (optional)
2 cups hot filtered water

1. In a heavy-duty blender on high speed, blend the cacao powder, hemp seeds, coconut oil, manuka honey, chicory root, reishi, cinnamon, cayenne, and filtered hot water until smooth (about 30 seconds to 1 minute).

TO SERVE: Pour in your favorite mug and get your day started!

DYK: Cayenne is a well-known digestive aid. It stimulates the digestive tract, increasing the flow of enzyme production and gastric juices. This aids the body's ability to metabolize food (and toxins).

DYK: Coconut oil is one of our favorite plant-based fats to use in our lives. It can boost fat burning in the body and provide your body and brain with quick energy.

BEVERAGES | 49

BEVERAGES

Oat Milk

Whoa! Oat milk has taken the plant-based world by storm! It seems like everyone is talking about it these days! It is the creamiest tasting milk we have ever had. We especially love it because it has a lower environmental impact on the planet than rice, almond, and soy milk. Contrary to nut milks, oat milk needs a fraction of the water that almonds do and is much more sustainable.

For this recipe, you can adjust the water. Use less than 4 cups, and it will become thicker and creamier. For granola, we like it thinner, but if we are making ice cream, we like it slightly thicker. We sometimes blend it 50/50 with Coconut Milk (page 52) or Cashew Milk (page 53) to change things up and get creative when we use it for lattes, cereals, and smoothies. It is so versatile and easy to make! ☺

PREP TIME: 5 minutes
MAKES: 4 cups
SHELF LIFE: 3 days in the fridge

4 cups filtered water
2 pitted dates
1 pinch sea salt
1 cup rolled oats
½ tsp vanilla

DYK: We love using Bob's Red Mill brand of gluten-free rolled oats for all of our oat-y needs!

1. In a heavy-duty blender on high speed, blend the water, dates, and salt until the dates are broken down, about 2 minutes.

2. Add the oats and blend on high speed for 45 seconds. Be sure to not overmix. It can make the milk slimy when over-blended.

3. To strain, place a nut milk bag over a large bowl. While holding the top, pour the oat-milk mixture into the bag or sieve, then gently squeeze the liquid through the bag. If you want virtually zero pulp, we recommend straining through a clean dishtowel or t-shirt.

4. Add vanilla to strained oat milk.

TO SERVE: Enjoy immediately or store in a glass jar in the fridge for up to 5 days.

Coconut Milk

When Kelly was in Ubud, Bali, everything was coconut (breakfast, lunch, and dinner), and she swears her body and health had never felt better. Coconut milk is one of our favorite plant-based milks. Its flavor works with everything from smoothies to soups and even ice cream! It also has natural gut-healing probiotics that keep your digestive system on track, and healthy fats to nourish your body. Use this milk in any recipe as a substitute for the other plant-based milks.

PREP TIME: 10 minutes
MAKES: 4 cups
SHELF LIFE: 3 days in the fridge

4 cups filtered water
1½ cups unsweetened shredded coconut
4 pitted dates
Pinch of sea salt
½ tsp vanilla (optional)

1. In a small saucepan, heat the filtered water over medium heat for about 5 minutes—until warm.

2. Add the warm water and coconut shreds to a heavy-duty blender and let sit for 3 minutes to soften. Then blend for about 1 minute on high speed until smooth.

3. To strain, place a nut milk bag over a large glass bowl. While holding the top of the bag, pour the coconut milk mixture into the bag, then gently squeeze the liquid through the bag.

4. Add dates, vanilla and sea salt to the coconut milk and blend on high until smooth.

TO SERVE: Enjoy immediately or store in a glass mason jar for up to 3 days in the fridge. If your milk develops a film, you can either shake it in your mason jar, or add it to your blender and blend until smooth.

NOTE: Using slightly warm water in this recipe helps the coconut shreds to soften and soak up as much water as possible.

Cashew Milk

Everyone needs a good, go-to plant-based milk, something that's quick and easy and doesn't break the bank. Did you know that making your own milk costs about 80 percent less than purchasing the store-bought ones? We love cashew milk. It's the easiest nut milk to make—so versatile, rich, creamy, and high in magnesium, zinc, and phosphorus for bone-building health!

PREP TIME: 10 minutes
SOAK TIME: 1 hour
MAKES: about 4 cups
SHELF LIFE: 3 days in the fridge

1 cup raw cashews

4 cups filtered water, plus extra for soaking

Pinch of sea salt

1. To soak the cashews, place them in a glass or ceramic bowl and fill with just enough filtered water to cover. Soak at room temperature for a minimum of 1 hour. We've been known to shorten the soaking time to 15 minutes if we're in a hurry.

2. Drain the cashews and rinse them several times with cold water.

3. Add the rinsed cashews, 4 cups filtered water, and sea salt to a heavy-duty blender. Blend on high speed until smooth, about 1 to 2 minutes. Unlike other plant based milks, cashew milk doesn't require straining after blending!

4. Enjoy immediately or store in a glass jar in the fridge for up to 3 days.

DYK: Cashews are full of healthy fats that can aid in lowering your cholesterol and blood pressure levels. We love them!

Detox Juice

We love the refreshing flavor of this juice. It's rich in vitamin C and beta carotene, which can help to keep your skin glowing. Carrots can work as a natural sunscreen too—from the inside out. Go ahead, protect your skin!

PREP TIME: 5 minutes
MAKES: 2 servings
SHELF LIFE: 2 days in the fridge

1 cup pineapple, peeled and diced

1 Tbsp fresh ginger

1 tsp fresh turmeric root (use ground turmeric in a pinch)

2 carrots, peeled

2 oranges, peeled

1 grapefruit, peeled

1. In the order they are listed, add the pineapple, ginger, turmeric root, carrots, oranges, and grapefruit to a juicer.

TO SERVE: Pour into a tall glass and drink immediately or store in an airtight container in the fridge for up to 2 days (stir before serving).

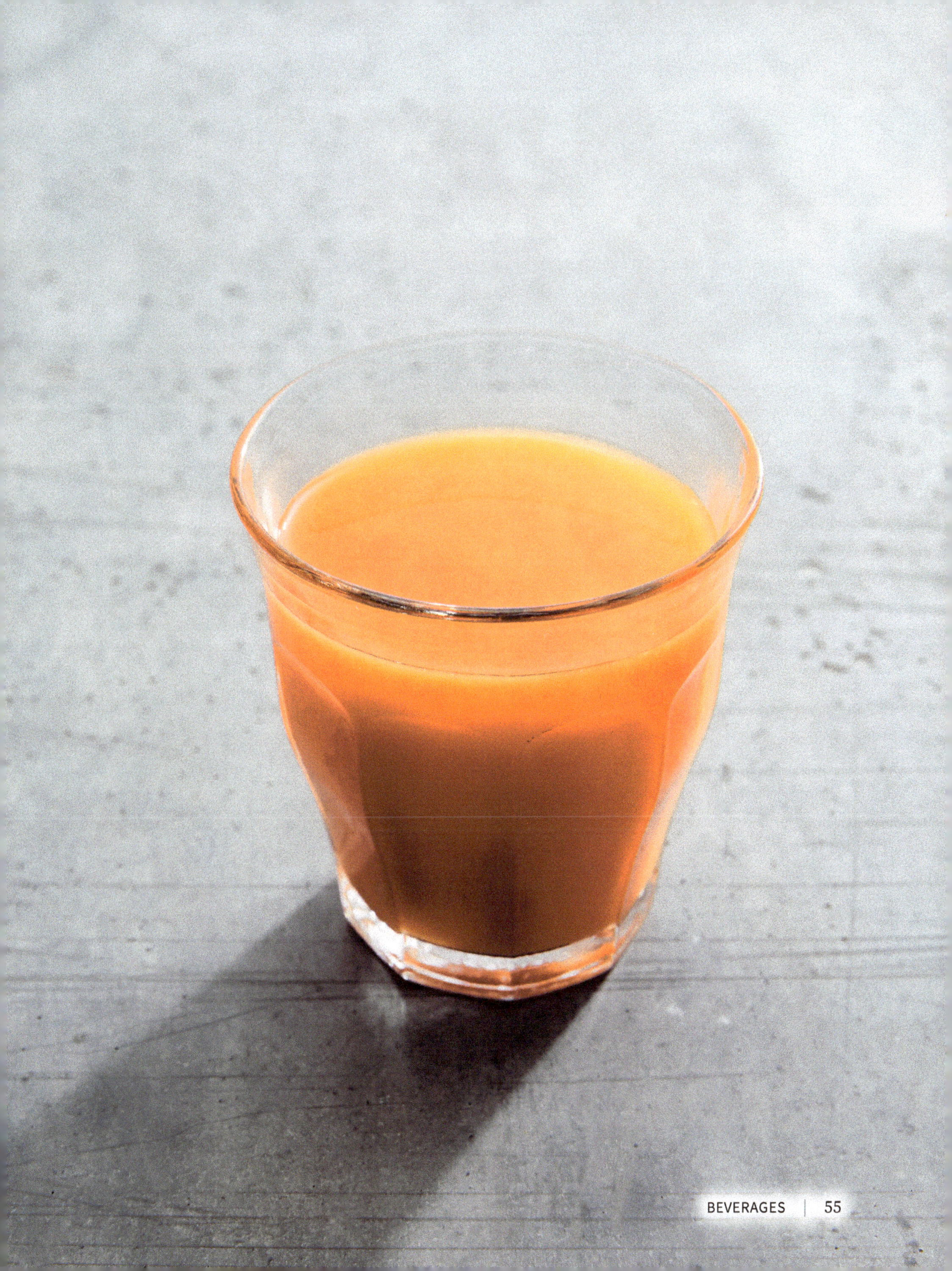

Digestive Tincture

We all can use this helpful tincture to assist with digestion after a meal. It benefits the body and soul. The more we learn about lemon balm, the more we LOVE it. It calms the body. It calms the nerves. It rids our bodies of unwanted bacteria. This tincture is potent, so we recommend drinking it immediately or using it within 48 hours.

WHITE PINE NEEDLE TEA (PAGE 71)

SOUL SOOTHING TURMERIC TONIC (PAGE 67)

DYK: Lemon balm can help relieve stress and anxiety. It's great before bed to lull you to sleep, and it also contains a compound called rosmarinic acid that appears to have potent antioxidant and antimicrobial properties.

PEPPERMINT TEA LEAVES

56 | BEVERAGES

KOMBUCHA

PREP TIME: 5 minutes
MAKES: 4 servings
SHELF LIFE: 2 days

1 Tbsp coconut oil
1 tsp grated ginger
1 dropper full of lemon balm tincture
1 tsp lemon juice
1 Tbsp Manuka honey or maple syrup
2 cups hot organic peppermint tea (teabags removed)

1. In a blender on high speed, blend the coconut oil, grated ginger, lemon balm, lemon juice, Manuka honey, and peppermint tea for 30 seconds.

2. Pour the mixture into a sealed mason jar and pull from (½ cup servings) as needed.

TO SERVE: Warm up on the stovetop prior to drinking and allow these beautiful ingredients to work their magic.

DIGESTIVE TINCTURE

BEVERAGES | 57

BEVERAGES

Black Lemonade

Activated charcoal is an incredibly powerful ingredient to add to juices and smoothies. Its absorption properties have superstar status. It will bind with toxins to pull them out of your body and help to detoxify and aid in digestion. It is also known to pull viruses, bacteria, fungi, and chemicals from water! Did you know that hospitals sometimes use activated charcoal for an overdose or poisoning? That's how powerful it is. Try this refreshing Black Lemonade to keep you hydrated and help give your body a cleansing once a week.

PREP TIME: 5 minutes
MAKES: 2 servings
SHELF LIFE: 2 days in the fridge

5 cups filtered water
⅓ cup maple syrup
1 cup fresh lemon juice
Pinch sea salt
2 tsp activated charcoal

1. In a large pitcher, stir together the filtered water, maple syrup, lemon juice, and sea salt.

2. Carefully add the charcoal and stir well until combined.

TO SERVE: Pour in a glass over ice, if desired.

NOTE: If you are pregnant or breastfeeding, consult a doctor before consuming activated charcoal.

Chia Agua Fresca

Who doesn't love a refreshing drink on a hot summer day? *Agua fresca* is Spanish for a "fresh water drink." It is very popular in Mexico, and we drink it every time we visit. This *agua fresca* is full of citrus and mint and is satisfying and full of the detoxing health benefits of chia seeds.

PREP TIME: 5 minutes
MAKES: 1 serving or 2 cups
SHELF LIFE: 2 days in the fridge

1 lime
2 cups filtered water
1 tsp mint, minced
½ tsp maple syrup
1 tsp chia seeds

1. Cut the lime in half. Peel one-half and set aside. Cut the other half into slices and reserve for the garnish.

2. In a blender on high speed, blend the filtered water, peeled lime, mint, and maple syrup for 30 seconds until combined.

3. Pour the juice into a glass mason jar.

4. Add the chia seeds and let sit for 5 to 10 minutes until the chia seeds start to become gelatinous. Shake every so often to ensure the chia seeds don't sink to the bottom.

TO SERVE: Pour in a tall glass and garnish with lime slices.

DYK: Chia seeds are rich in fiber, antioxidants, and omega-3 fatty acids. They have been known to keep your digestive tract and brain happy!

BEVERAGES

BEVERAGES

Simple Green

A more palatable way to get your celery and other greens is with this powerhouse green juice. Filled with so many micronutrients, it's the perfect way to start your day. Cilantro removes heavy metals from your body! Kale is high in protein! Spinach is high in iron! Pineapple is anti-inflammatory!

PREP TIME: 5 minutes
MAKES: 1 serving
SHELF LIFE: 2 days in the fridge

1 cup kale
2 green apples, cut in half
1 cup spinach
3 stalks celery
2 Tbsp fresh mint
2 Tbsp fresh cilantro or basil
½ cup peeled and cored pineapple

1. In the order they are listed, add the kale, the first apple, spinach, celery, mint, cilantro, the next apple, and pineapple to a juicer.

TO SERVE: Pour in a glass to drink now, or store in a glass jar in the fridge for up to 2 days.

DYK: Leafy green vegetables are packed full of healthy vitamins and minerals but are low in calories. To get the full spectrum of health benefits that these powerhouses offer, be sure to add a wide variety of leafy greens to your diet.

BEVERAGES | 63

Celery Juice

Celery is an herb! It is not a vegetable. It rids us of toxins and fuels wellness on a whole new level. Kelly can speak firsthand about the healing power of celery juice while dealing with a chronic infection.

PREP TIME: 3 minutes
MAKES: 1 serving or 16 ounces (2 cups)
SHELF LIFE: Immediate preferred, but up to 24 hours in the fridge

1 head of celery (stem removed and rinsed thoroughly)

1. Add the celery to the juicer.

2. Serve immediately or cover well and refrigerate for the next 6–12 hours.

TO SERVE: Daily serving size is 16 ounces. Celery juice must be consumed on an empty stomach, and also, do not eat or drink anything for 30–45 minutes after you consume your juice.

DYK: Celery has a very special molecular configuration of unique cluster salts that are unlike any other food on the planet. It is known to purify the liver and the fats and toxins built up in it that can lead to so many chronic illnesses. We've learned so much from Anthony William, The Medical Medium, be sure to check out his work on the healing power of celery juice. The optimal way to get the most healing powers from celery is from straight celery juice (not blended in a smoothie or eaten with Cheez Whiz on it! JUST CELERY JUICE)

BEVERAGES | 65

BEVERAGES

Soul-Soothing Turmeric Tonic

Turmeric is an incredible antioxidant that helps reduce inflammation and detoxify the body. Have this tonic as part of your morning ritual to give your body the love it deserves!

PREP TIME: 3 minutes
COOK TIME: 15 minutes
MAKES: 2 servings
SHELF LIFE: 5 days in the fridge

1 Tbsp fresh turmeric

1 Tbsp fresh grated ginger

Juice of 1 lemon

4 drops echinacea or white pine needle tincture

1 tsp maple syrup

3 cups filtered water

1. Add the turmeric, ginger, lemon juice, echinacea or white pine tincture, maple syrup, and filtered water to a small saucepan.

2. Bring to a simmer over medium-low heat and cook for 5 minutes. Turn the heat off and let sit for 15 minutes—the longer it sits, the better.

3. Set a small strainer over a serving glass and pour the tonic and strain. Repeat.

TO SERVE: Pour in a glass. Store leftovers in the fridge for up to 5 days.

NOTE: You can make this more concentrated by tripling the ingredients except for the water. Then combine ⅓ cup of the tonic with ⅔ cup of hot water. This way you have it throughout the week with ease.

DYK: Turmeric has been known to reduce inflammation in the body and provides the body with more antioxidants, which help to fight off illness and keep the body healthy! During cold and flu season, drink this every day! Echinacea is optional but worth it to help to prevent colds from grabbing hold of us.

BEVERAGES

Wellness Shot

Erinn is obsessed with ginger. The more she eats, the more she craves it. Ginger is an incredible addition to your daily lifestyle, and we eat a lot of it. It's incredible for your immune system! Ginger also helps you digest food. We've created this wellness shot with refreshing, anti-bloating, and detoxifying apple cider vinegar to give you a jump start to your day. It is like setting an intention to have an amazing day in the best way possible.

PREP TIME: 5 minutes
MAKES: 2 shots
SHELF LIFE: 2 days in the fridge

¼ cup fresh ginger
2 lemons, peeled
1 tsp apple cider vinegar

1. Add the ginger and lemon to a juicer.
2. Add the apple cider vinegar to the mixture.

TO SERVE: Pour into a shot glass and enjoy! Save the rest for tomorrow morning!

BEVERAGES | 69

BEVERAGES

White Pine Needle Tea

We talked about the infinite benefits of white pine needles in our Superfoods section of the book. Some of these included having a high vitamin C content and keeping your immune system thriving and vibrant.

PREP TIME: 3 minutes
MAKES: 1 serving

1 white pine needle teabag
(We love Muskoka Girls Tea & Stonehouse Holistics.)

1. Heat filtered water in a kettle until boiled. Using a mug, pour the hot water over the pine needle teabag and let steep for 5-10 minutes.

2. Reuse the teabag 3–4 times to get all of the goodness out of it.

DYK: You can also make your own tea by using eastern white pine needles that you may have on your property and placing them in a steeper or cloth teabag. Just please make sure that it's the correct type of pine tree you're using. We also purchase white pine tincture from Stonehouse Holistics and take two dropperfuls a day for optimal health.

BEVERAGES | 71

MORINGA POWDER—very powerful adaptogen, known specifically for fighting stress and sleeplessness.

CORDYCEPS MUSHROOMS—are known to stimulate the adrenal system and help to regulate cortisol levels (aka stress levels!).

MACA — helps to boost the immune system and balance hormones.

Adaptogens

Adaptogens are plants and mushrooms that help your body respond in a health way to stress, fatigue and anxiety. We take adaptogens in powder, capsule or elixir form most often. Many of these are available at your local health food store!

ASHWAGANDHA — is an **ayurvedic herb**. It has been used to combat and reduce stress and thereby enhance general wellbeing. We add it to smoothies!

74

Smoothies and Smoothie Bowls

Date Shake 76

Golden Mylkshake 79

Hormone Balancing Smoothie 80

Pura Vida Smoothie 81

Sunrise Smoothie 82

Sweet Potato Smoothie 85

The Palm Springs Smoothie 86

Eternal Glow Bowl 88

Green Goddess Smoothie Bowl 91

Mermaid Bowl 92

Date Shake

We found our first "date shake" (aka smoothie!) in Palm Springs (the center of our Universe), California, back in 2006. We weren't plant-based at the time, but when we tried this smoothie, which tastes more like a milkshake, it was like we had died and gone to heaven! Ever since then, we go back to Palm Springs every year (sometimes two to three times a year!), and the first thing we do is order DATE SHAKES for the FAM!

PREP TIME: 5 minutes
MAKES: 1 serving

1½ frozen bananas

3 Medjool dates, pitted

1 ½ cup Coconut Milk (page 52), Cashew Milk (page 53), or store-bought canned coconut milk

1. In a heavy-duty blender, on high speed, blend the banana, dates, and coconut milk until smooth (about 1 minute).

TO SERVE: Enjoy in a tall glass.

TIP: If your dates are a little dry, we recommend soaking them in warm water for 10–15 minutes before using.

SMOOTHIES AND SMOOTHIE BOWLS | 77

SMOOTHIES AND SMOOTHIE BOWLS

Golden Mylkshake

We love our turmeric! We created our own mylkshake with it that's thick and creamy and packs a ton of flavor and nutrition. Turmeric, also known as curcumin, is an anti-inflammatory healing powerhouse!

PREP TIME: 5 minutes
MAKES: 1 large serving or 2 small servings

1 cup canned coconut milk

¾ cup Oat Milk (page 51) or store-bought

2 frozen bananas

1 tsp ground or fresh turmeric

½ tsp cinnamon

1 Tbsp almond butter

¼ cup shredded coconut

2 Tbsp chia seeds

¼ tsp vanilla extract

1 tsp cordyceps mushroom powder (see DYK, page 46)

Pinch of black pepper

½ cup ice

1. In a heavy-duty blender, on high speed, blend the coconut milk, oat milk, bananas, turmeric, cinnamon, almond butter, shredded coconut, chia seeds, vanilla, cordyceps mushrooms, black pepper, and ice until smooth. About 1 minute.

TO SERVE: Enjoy in a tall glass. Turmeric is so good!

Hormone Balancing Smoothie

Hormone health is such an integral part of all of our lives. We believe in balancing hormones at any age. By using incredible superfoods like ashwagandha and maca, you'll feel more balanced, less stressed, and happier overall. This is a very basic flavor smoothie, but it packs a punch in terms of health benefits. Feel free to add a tablespoon of cacao or a handful of raspberries if you want to jazz this smoothie up.

PREP TIME: 5 minutes
MAKES: 1 serving

1½ cups Coconut Milk (page 52)

1 frozen banana

½ avocado, pitted and peeled

1 tsp maca

1 tsp ashwagandha powder or elixir (see DYK, page 44)

½ tsp lion's mane elixir (see DYK, page 46)

½ Tbsp coconut oil

1 tsp vanilla

1. In a heavy-duty blender, on high speed, blend the coconut milk, banana, avocado, maca, ashwagandha, lion's mane, coconut oil, and vanilla until smooth (about 1 minute).

TO SERVE: Enjoy in a tall glass and begin to feel the calm.

DYK: We need to nourish our bodies to have a better connection to our soul. If we don't eat right and are full of toxins and other things that can cause "aggravation" within the body, it is very difficult to meditate and be connected to joy. Remember, we ARE what we eat. This is a new lifestyle for you, incorporating new ways of nourishing your body and soul. Allow these superfoods time to build up in your body. Sometimes it takes about two weeks to feel the true effects of maca or ashwagandha.

Pura Vida Smoothie

Traveling in magical Nosara, Costa Rica, was an incredible journey. We were able to meet some fascinating people, eat delicious local food, and do some pretty crazy stuff, like surfing in the warm Pacific Ocean and zip-lining in the jungle! AHHH!! This smoothie was one of our favorites during our stay.

PREP TIME: 5 minutes
MAKES: 1 serving

½ avocado, pitted and peeled

1 cup peeled and frozen pineapple chunks

½ frozen banana

½ tsp ground turmeric

1 cup coconut water

½ cup ice

1. In a heavy-duty blender, on high speed, blend the avocado, pineapple, banana, turmeric, coconut water, and ice until smooth (about 1 minute). If it's a little thick for your liking, feel free to add a little more coconut water.

TO SERVE: Enjoy in a tall glass and dream you are in Costa Rica, then go and seize the day!

DYK: Costa Rica is noted as one of the "Blue Zones" of the world. Blue Zones are areas where the average lifespan is much longer than in the rest of the world. In Costa Rica, it's about ninety years old! They spend the time to create special connections to one another in their communities, and they live closely together in family units, eating very healthy with locally grown crops.

Sunrise Smoothie

This was one of Erinn's favorite smoothies during her travels in Kauai, Hawaii. It's inspired by the coffee shop Java Kai. Who would have thought that raw beets would work in a smoothie? This is such a yummy powerhouse of nutrition! Raw beets help to bring oxygen into your blood and an uplifting of energy into your day.

PREP TIME: 5 minutes
MAKES: 2 servings

1 cup peeled papaya
2 frozen bananas, diced
¼ cup peeled and diced red beets
1-inch ginger, peeled
1 cup Coconut Milk (page 52)
½ cup fresh carrot juice
2 Tbsp maple syrup

1. In a heavy-duty blender, blend the papaya, bananas, red beets, ginger, coconut milk, carrot juice, and maple syrup until smooth, about 1–2 minutes.

TO SERVE: Enjoy in a tall glass or store in a sealed glass mason jar and shake before drinking. Take a deep breath, feel the energy come through you, and enjoy the sunrise.

SMOOTHIES AND SMOOTHIE BOWLS | 83

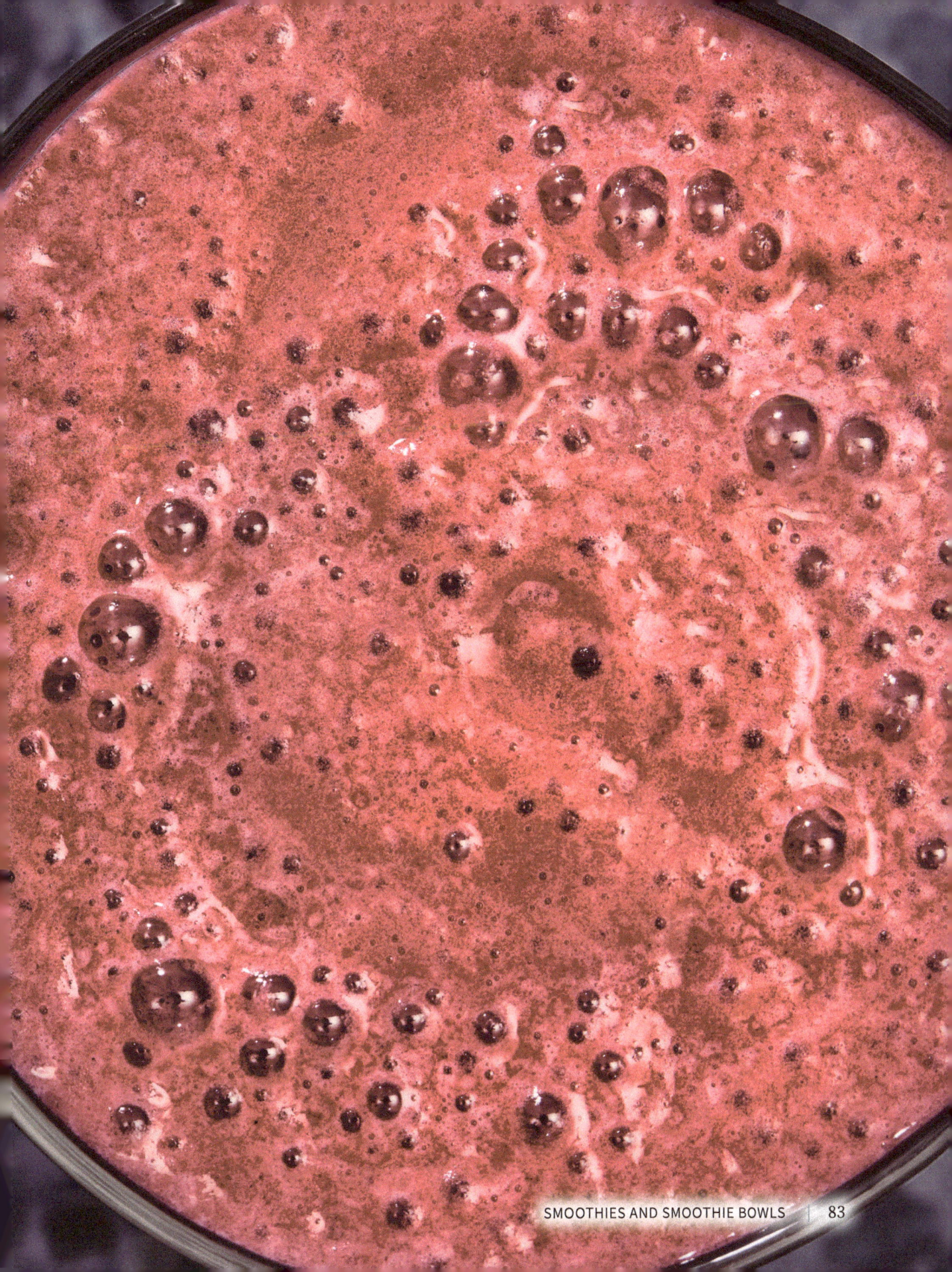

SMOOTHIES AND SMOOTHIE BOWLS

Sweet Potato Smoothie

Our Kindfood Cafe followers loved this back in the day because it embodied "comfort food." It's such a wonderfully satisfying smoothie for any time of the year (especially the fall and winter). The rich and earthy flavor, reminiscent of sweet potato pie, makes you just feel like you're indulging. But, in fact, you're not! It is so good for you!

PREP TIME: 5 minutes
MAKES: 1–2 servings

1 cup organic diced and cooked (then cooled) sweet potato or canned sweet potato

1½ cups Coconut Milk (page 52)

1 frozen banana

½ avocado, peeled and pitted

2 Tbsp maple syrup

2 tsp coconut oil

1 tsp vanilla extract

½ tsp cinnamon

½ tsp nutmeg

½ tsp allspice

1. In a heavy-duty blender, blend the sweet potato, coconut milk, banana, avocado, maple syrup, coconut oil, vanilla, cinnamon, nutmeg, and allspice until smooth (about 1–2 minutes).

TO SERVE: Enjoy in a tall glass and settle into the cozy vibes.

DYK: Adding avocado to smoothies is one of our tricks to instantly make it rich and creamy.

The Palm Springs Smoothie

When we first started going to Palm Springs, California (one of our favorite places to go as a family), we stumbled upon a sweet little café called Palm Greens Café. It served amazing smoothies and the most incredible healthy brunch. This smoothie is inspired by our time there. Every time we make it, we are brought back to the specialness of Palm Springs.

PREP TIME: 5 minutes
MAKES: 1 serving

2 frozen bananas
1 cup lightly packed spinach
½ cup lightly packed kale, stems removed
1½ cup coconut water
½ cup chopped apple
1 tsp chopped fresh ginger
1 Tbsp chopped fresh mint
1 tsp spirulina powder

1. In a heavy-duty blender, on high speed, blend the bananas, spinach, kale, coconut water, apple, ginger, mint, and spirulina until smooth (about 1 minute).

TO SERVE: Enjoy in a tall glass and envision you're sitting by a pool in Palm Springs!

DYK: If you're ever in Palm Springs, you have to check out the hiking trails! And Joshua Tree National Park! They are magnificent! There is a strong spiritual vortex in Palm Springs that brings a whole new level of energy within your soul when you visit there.

SMOOTHIES AND SMOOTHIE BOWLS | 87

Eternal Glow Bowl

This bowl is packed full of healthy vitamins! Yep, it will make your skin glow from the inside out! Before going away to a sunny destination, we always load up on all things full of beta-carotene as it acts as a natural sunscreen.

This bowl is also great for your gorgeous eyes too! Eye health is a real concern with all the digital work we do in front of the blue-light screens on our laptops and cell phones. If we load ourselves up with the best food possible, we can create a defensive front and protect our precious eyes.

PREP TIME: 5 minutes
MAKES: 1 serving

½ cup carrot, finely grated
1 cup butternut squash puree or sweet potato puree
1½ cup frozen mango chunks
¼ cup Coconut Milk (page 52) or store-bought
1 tsp turmeric powder
1-inch knob ginger root, peeled (about 1 Tbsp chopped)
½ tsp cinnamon
¼ tsp cardamom
Pinch of sea salt
Pinch of black pepper

SUGGESTED TOPPINGS:

2 Tbsp coconut flakes
5–6 almonds
3 Tbsp fresh blueberries
Handful of granola of your choice

1. In a heavy-duty blender, on high speed, blend the carrot, butternut squash, mango, coconut milk, turmeric, ginger, cinnamon, cardamom, sea salt, and black pepper until smooth and creamy (about 30 seconds to 1 minute).

TO SERVE: Pour into a bowl, add your favorite toppings, and enjoy with a (large) spoon.

NOTE: This is a thick smoothie recipe so feel free to add more liquid as required, a little at a time. We use a narrow spatula to push the smoothie down to ensure it is fully blended.

SAVORY OPTION: If you'd like to create a less sweet, savory smoothie, simply omit the mango and blend all of the remaining ingredients.

DYK: Adding black pepper to this smoothie can help the body absorb the anti-inflammatory properties of turmeric; combining the spices magnifies their effects.

SMOOTHIES AND SMOOTHIE BOWLS | 89

SMOOTHIES AND SMOOTHIE BOWLS

Green Goddess Smoothie Bowl

Enjoy this delicious and refreshing bowl for a well-balanced breakfast or as an afternoon snack. We've added almond butter to this recipe for an additional protein kick and creaminess!

PREP TIME: 5 minutes
MAKES: 1 serving

2 frozen bananas

¼ cup unsweetened canned coconut milk

1 cup lightly packed spinach

1 kiwi, peeled

2 Tbsp almond butter or small handful of almonds

SUGGESTED TOPPINGS:

2 Tbsp shredded coconut (we prefer the unsweetened kind!)

1 handful of chopped almonds

½ banana, sliced

1 kiwi, sliced

1 Tbsp hemp seeds

1 tsp chia seeds

1. In a heavy-duty blender, on high speed, blend the banana, coconut milk, spinach, kiwi, and almond butter until smooth (for about 30 seconds).

TO SERVE: Pour into a bowl, add your desired toppings, and embrace your inner goddess.

NOTE: This is a thick smoothie recipe so feel free to add more liquid as required, a little at a time. We use a narrow spatula to push the smoothie down to ensure it is fully blended.

Mermaid Bowl

Who doesn't want to feel like a mermaid? Spirulina is high in protein and also improves the look and feel of your skin. It gives you a boost of energy too! Did we mention this smoothie bowl is beautiful to look at? (Especially if you use the Blue Majik—ohhhhhh, that blue!) Your kids will love this playful-looking smoothie bowl and will have no idea how healthy it is for them. The great thing about kids and smoothie bowls is that your kids can get in on the decorating! To make this smoothie bowl extra rich and creamy, use canned organic coconut milk.

PREP TIME: 5 minutes
MAKES: 1 serving

1 frozen banana

1 avocado, peeled and pitted

¼ cup Coconut Milk (page 52) or canned coconut milk

1 kiwi, peeled

1 tsp spirulina powder or Blue Majik™ (see DYK)

SUGGESTED TOPPINGS:

2 Tbsp fresh blueberries

1 Tbsp chopped mint leaves

1 tsp cacao nibs

½ tsp bee pollen

1 Tbsp flaked coconut

1. In a heavy-duty blender, on high speed, blend the banana, avocado, coconut milk, kiwi, and spirulina powder until smooth (about 30 seconds).

NOTE: This is a thick smoothie recipe so feel free to add more liquid as required, a little at a time. We use a narrow spatula to push the smoothie down to ensure it is fully blended.

TO SERVE: Pour into a bowl, add your desired toppings, and make some smoothie bowl art!

DYK: Spirulina and Blue Majik are types of superfood algae with antioxidants that can help lower blood pressure. They are also known to have strong hormone healing effects!

SMOOTHIES AND SMOOTHIE BOWLS | 93

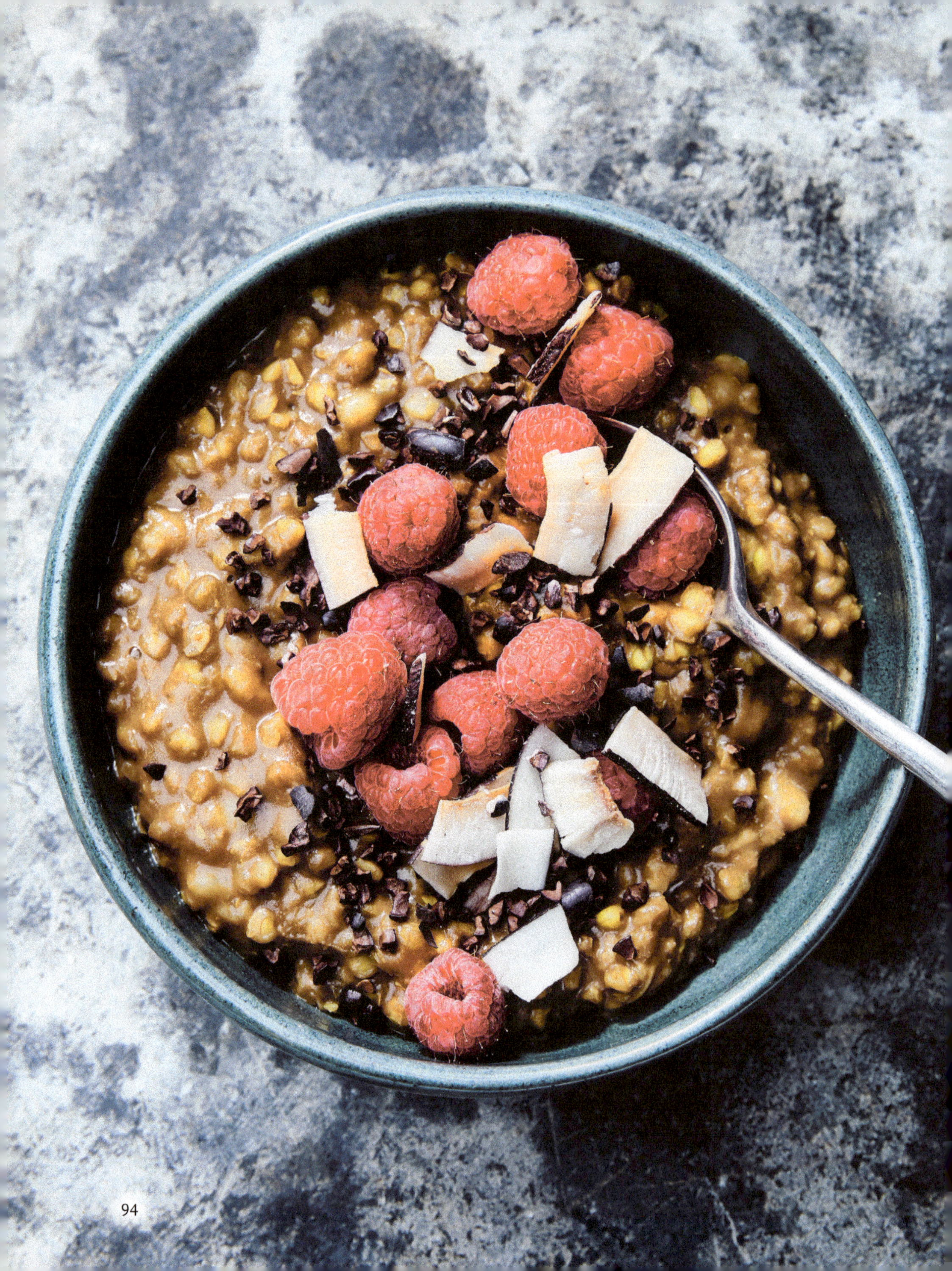

Breakfast

Banana Bread Superfood Granola　96

The Choco Bowl　99

Kelly & Erinn's Superfood Raw-Nola　100

Sweet Potato Porridge　103

Creamsicle Clementine Chia Pudding　104

Lemon "Cheesecake" Chia Pudding　107

Sweet Potato Toasts　108

Wild Blueberry Chia Jam　111

Coconut Yogurt　112

Fat Bombs　115

Raspberry Cloud Chia Pudding　116

Pumpkin Waffles　119

Savory Breakfast Bowl　123

Toasts with Avocado　124

Banana Bread Superfood Granola

We love everything about granola, a nutritious comfort food. It tastes like one of our favorite things: banana bread! YUMMMMMMM! For the perfect breakfast, serve it with some of our Cashew Milk (page 53) or Oat Milk (page 51), sliced bananas, and fresh blueberries. It even tastes incredible when it is warm from the oven! Back off! Gimme a handful!

PREP TIME: 15 minutes
BAKE TIME: 30 minutes
MAKES: 8–10 servings
SHELF LIFE: 2 weeks in the fridge or 1 month in the freezer

4 cups gluten-free rolled oats
2 tsp cinnamon
¾ cup roughly chopped raw walnuts
½ cup roughly chopped raw pecans
¼ cup roughly chopped raw almonds
3 Tbsp coconut sugar
½ tsp sea salt
1 Tbsp flaxseeds
2 Tbsp chia seeds
1 tsp maca powder
⅓ cup coconut oil
¼ cup maple syrup
1 tsp vanilla extract
1 ripe banana, peeled and mashed
½ cup vegan chocolate chips (optional)

1. Preheat oven to 350°F, and line a baking sheet with parchment paper.

2. In a large bowl, combine the rolled oats, cinnamon, walnuts, pecans, almonds, coconut sugar, sea salt, flaxseeds, chia seeds, and maca powder.

3. In a small saucepan over medium heat, warm the coconut oil, maple syrup, and vanilla extract. Once melted, remove from heat, add the mashed banana, and stir until combined.

4. Add the banana mixture to the oat mixture and stir until all pieces are coated.

5. Bake for 30 minutes; tossing halfway through. It's done when it's nice and golden brown.

6. Remove from the oven and let cool. Stir in chocolate chips if using.

TO SERVE: Pour 1 cup of granola into a bowl and top with your favorite non-dairy milk, or yogurt and get your day started!

BREAKFAST | 97

BREAKFAST

The Choco Bowl

Breakfast bowls are so yummy. In addition to being nutrient-dense, the Choco Bowl is also naturally sweetened with bananas and rich with superfood antioxidants, thanks to cacao powder and turmeric. (Who knew that they work well together?) Fresh raspberries, cacao nibs, sliced bananas, toasted nuts, toasted sunflower seeds, and/or coconut make the perfect topping. So much to choose from and all easily found in your local health-food store.

PREP TIME: 5 minutes
COOK TIME: 15 minutes
MAKES: 1 serving
SHELF LIFE: 2 days in the fridge

1 cup Oat Milk (page 51), divided
⅓ cup buckwheat groats, well-rinsed
¼ tsp cacao powder
½ tsp turmeric powder
1 large banana, mashed
Pinch of sea salt
Pinch of ground black pepper

SUGGESTED TOPPINGS:

1 Tbsp raspberries
1 tsp cacao nibs
1 tsp shredded coconut
Sprinkle of toasted sunflower seeds
Additional plant-based milk of your choice

1. In a small saucepan, bring ½ cup of oat milk to a boil.

2. Add the buckwheat, cacao powder, and turmeric, reduce the heat to simmer, and cook until almost all the liquid has been absorbed (about 10 minutes), stirring occasionally.

3. Add the mashed banana, another ½ cup of oat milk, sea salt, and black pepper. Cook until the banana has fully combined (another 5 minutes).

TO SERVE: Enjoy in a bowl and add your desired toppings.

NOTE: If keeping refrigerated for the next day, don't add the toppings until time of serving.

> **DYK:** Cacao is the raw, unprocessed form of cocoa. It has not been heated. It is very nutritious and vitally healthy for our bodies. It has 400x as many antioxidants as cocoa!

Kelly and Erinn's Superfood Raw-Nola

You can eat this raw-nola right out of the jar, soak it overnight with some vegan milk, or top it with berries for a delicious breakfast. We like it every way! This is a great granola to have on the go, whether it's for traveling to and from work, heading to soccer practice, or eating on the dock at the cottage. Note: Feel free to substitute in almonds, cashews. or other nuts you may love!

PREP TIME: 7–10 minutes
MAKES: about 4 cups, 10+ servings
SHELF LIFE: 2 weeks in the freezer

1 ¼ cup raw walnuts
1 cup raw almonds
20 pitted dates
1 Tbsp flaxseed meal
2 tsp chia seeds
⅓ cup unsweetened shredded coconut
⅔ cup gluten-free rolled oats (we like to use Bob's Red Mill!)
½ tsp cinnamon
½ tsp maca powder
½ tsp ashwagandha powder
2 Tbsp hemp seeds
½ tsp sea salt

SUGGESTED TOPPINGS (PER SERVING):

1 Tbsp dried fruit
¼ cup Coconut Milk (page 52)
1 tsp maple syrup
Small handful of chopped fresh fruit or berries of your choice
¼ cup Coconut Yogurt (page 112) or store-bought
Small handful cacao nibs

1. Add the walnuts and almonds to a food processor and pulse a few times to roughly chop. Add the dates and pulse to make a loose "dough" (about 30 seconds).

2. Add the flaxseed meal, chia seeds, shredded coconut, rolled oats, cinnamon, maca, ashwagandha, hemp seeds, and sea salt, and pulse to combine.

3. Enjoy as breakfast, a light snack right away, or store in an airtight container in the freezer.

TO SERVE: Have it on the go with your favorite toppings! Why not try some cashew milk and wild blueberries on top?

BREAKFAST | 101

102 | BREAKFAST

Sweet Potato Porridge

This recipe was inspired by one of our incredible trips to California—Santa Monica to be exact. We traveled there for a girls' trip and indulged in some incredible food along the way. This includes a version of this recipe at the Flower Child restaurant. Erinn had it almost every day we were there! She was nuts for it! WARNING: You may become addicted too.

PREP TIME: 5 minutes
COOK TIME: 15 minutes
MAKES: 4 servings
SHELF LIFE: 2 days in the fridge

2 cups filtered water

1 cup of sweet potato puree

¾ cup Coconut Milk (page 52) or store-bought coconut milk

1 Tbsp vanilla extract

¼ cup maple syrup

1 tsp cinnamon

1 tsp nutmeg

⅛ tsp sea salt

¾ cup white quinoa, rinsed and drained

¾ cup gluten-free rolled oats

SUGGESTED TOPPINGS (PER SERVING):

1 Tbsp Whipped Cream (page 242)

2 Tbsp Cashew Milk (page 53)

Small handful toasted pecans

¼ banana, sliced

1. In a medium saucepan over medium heat, mix the water, sweet potato puree, coconut milk, vanilla, maple syrup, cinnamon, nutmeg, and sea salt. Bring to a boil.

2. Add the quinoa and oats. Lower heat to simmer, covered, for about 12 to 15 minutes, until about 90 percent of all liquid is absorbed.

3. Serve warm and top with suggested toppings. Enjoy.

BREAKFAST

Creamsicle Clementine Chia Pudding

"Oh, my goodness! OMG! OMG!" That's all we can say about this recipe. When we gave a sample to our friends, they all went CRAZY for it! Even the pickiest of eaters LOVED it! With no added sugar, everyone will think it's a real treat, and you will definitely fool them. It is deceivingly healthy. We love clementines, and this way we can celebrate them when they are in season in the winter, while we also get our vitamin C.

This recipe can work with oranges, if need be, but the remarkably unique sweetness of clementines makes this pudding the most memorable.

PREP TIME: 10 minutes
CHILL TIME: 2 hours
MAKES: 4 large or 8 snack-size servings
SHELF LIFE: 3 days in the fridge

3 cups clementine orange segments
1 (13.5 oz) can full-fat coconut milk
3 Tbsp filtered water
½ cup chia seeds
1 cup unsweetened coconut shavings
1 cup clementine (or orange) segments for garnish

1. In a high-speed blender, blend the clementine segments, coconut milk, and filtered water until completely smooth (about 1 minute).

2. Pour mixture into a large glass storage container and add the chia seeds. Cover and shake well to combine and then chill in the fridge for at least 2 hours to set.

3. Remove from the fridge and layer your clementine pudding at the bottom of a mason jar, alternating between clementine segments, coconut shavings, and chia pudding.

TO SERVE: Using a spoon, eat directly from the mason jar. This is the perfect mid-afternoon snack or breakfast.

BREAKFAST | 105

BREAKFAST

Lemon "Cheesecake" Chia Pudding

Who wants lemon cheesecake for breakfast? Oh my gosh! WE DO!!!! We love the versatility of this recipe—meaning it is great for breakfast or as a special dessert! Lemon works really well in the morning to wake up our taste buds and at the end of a meal to cleanse our palettes. We also love the taste of Meyer lemons in this recipe, and if you can find them, choose these first! Pucker up!

PREP TIME: 5 minutes
CHILL TIME: 1 hour
MAKES: 2 servings
SHELF LIFE: 2 days in the fridge

2 lemons, zested and juiced
1 (14 oz) can full-fat coconut milk
¼ cup maple syrup
¼ cup raw cashews
⅓ cup white or black chia seeds

1. In a heavy-duty blender, on high speed, blend the zest and juice of lemons, coconut milk, maple syrup, and raw cashews until smooth (about 1 minute).

2. In a large mason jar, add the blended mixture and the chia seeds, and stir or shake to combine.

3. Refrigerate for a minimum of 1 hour.

TO SERVE: Eat this "cheesecake" right out of the jar or pour into a bowl and save the rest for later.

DYK: You can find white chia seeds at your local health-food store. Feel free to use white or black chia seeds.

BREAKFAST | 107

Sweet Potato Toasts

Sweet potato toast.... SAY WHAT?! It has way more health benefits than traditional toast, and we guarantee it will keep you fuller longer with its complex carbohydrate benefits. The key is to have a sharp knife to make the slices as uniform as possible.

PREP TIME: 10 minutes
MAKES: 4–6 slices
SHELF LIFE: Serve immediately

TOAST

1 large sweet potato

Desired topping (see variations below)

1. Slice the sweet potato lengthwise into four to six ¼-inch-thick slices, depending on the size of the sweet potato. Be careful to make the cuts as even as possible.

2. Toast the sweet potato slices on high heat in your toaster until cooked through, about 5 to 10 minutes. You may need to toast multiple times depending on your toaster.

3. Meanwhile, prepare your desired spread.

TO SERVE: Spread the topping on the potato slice and enjoy. Toast be gone!

VARIATION 1: ALMOND MACA BUTTER

⅓ cup almond butter

2 tsp maca powder

2 tsp maple syrup

1. In a small bowl, combine the almond butter, maca, and maple syrup.

2. Top the sweet potato toasts with your almond maca butter and enjoy.

VARIATION 2: AVOCADO LIME

1 avocado, peeled and sliced

1 Tbsp lime juice

2–4 pinches sea salt

1. In a small bowl, add the avocado slices and lime juice. With a fork, mash up the avocado with the lime juice. Stir to combine.

2. Top your sweet potato toast with your avocado mixture and a pinch of sea salt.

BREAKFAST

BREAKFAST

Wild Blueberry Chia Jam

When we think of wild blueberries, we think about summer and eating them in Prince Edward County, Ontario. It's always fun taking a country drive and finding a local fruit stand selling them when they're in season. We made this jam as a quick alternative to store-bought jam, with this one having tons of added health benefits and no pectin.

Wild blueberries are a superfood. There is nothing like them. Do not confuse them with their larger, cultivated cousin. Wild blueberries are one of the most powerful brain foods we know, and one of the most effective heavy metal detoxing foods out there. And of course, if wild blueberries aren't in season, check the freezer department at your local grocery store. We bet you'll find them there. Use this jam for a delicious topping on Sweet Potato Porridge (page 103) or Waffles (page 119).

PREP TIME: 5 minutes
COOK TIME: 35–40 minutes
MAKES: 1 cup
SHELF LIFE: 5 days in the fridge or 2 months in the freezer in a small mason jar filled ⅔ to the top

3 cups fresh (or frozen) wild blueberries
2 Tbsp maple syrup
1 orange
1 tsp lemon juice
4 Tbsp chia seeds

1. In a small saucepan, over medium heat, add the blueberries and maple syrup, and heat for about 15 minutes. Reduce the heat to low and simmer for 10 minutes.

2. Meanwhile, cut the orange in half, and using a juice press (or the strength of your hand), juice the whole orange until you have about ½ cup.

3. Add the orange juice and lemon juice to the blueberry mixture and simmer on low for another 7–10 minutes, until about 25 percent of the liquid evaporates.

4. Add the chia seeds and mix until combined. Allow the jam to thicken on the stove for another 5 minutes.

5. Place in a small glass mason jar and allow to cool before storing in the fridge. This will keep for 5 days in the fridge.

Coconut Yogurt

Making your own coconut yogurt is super easy and allows you to decide what ingredients you are putting in your body. When you make your own healthy yogurt at home, you stay away from many of the preservatives and thickeners in store-bought brands. We like to make ours plain and then add a sweetener—maybe some Manuka honey, wild blueberries or Wild Blueberry Chia Jam (page 111).

PREP TIME: 5 minutes
FERMENTING TIME: 2 days
MAKES: 2 servings
SHELF LIFE: 4–7 days in fridge

1 can (14 oz) of full-fat coconut milk
2 vegan probiotic capsules

ADD-ONS:

Sweetener (Manuka honey, maple syrup, stevia, coconut nectar), blueberries, raspberries. Chia jam can be swirled in there too!

Banana Bread Superfood Granola (page 96)

1. Shake your coconut milk well! Ensure that it's very smooth and not clumpy. If you want to be extra certain everything has been combined, you can also use a high powered blender on high for 30 seconds.

2. Pour into a large sterilized mason jar. Sprinkle your probiotic capsules into the coconut milk and stir with a wooden spoon. (Please do not use metal, as it will react and change the activation of the probiotics.) Stir until creamy and smooth, ensuring the probiotic capsules are mixed thoroughly and all clumps are broken up.

3. Cover the mixture with a cheesecloth or dishtowel to let the air circulate and secure with a rubber band.

4. Let the yogurt activate for at least 24 hours, and up to 48 hours in a warm place where it won't be disturbed. (We leave ours on top of the refrigerator.)

5. Once the yogurt has the right consistency and has thickened, cover securely with a lid, and refrigerate until cold. This yogurt will thicken more with refrigeration—just like magic!

TO SERVE: Stir in wild blueberries and chia jam and drizzle with Manuka honey or maple syrup.

BREAKFAST | 113

BREAKFAST

Fat Bombs

As a health-conscious society, we've been told that fat is bad and will clog arteries and make you unhealthy. Well, when we talk about fat in this book, we're talking about all of the incredible healthy fats that are necessary to fuel your cells and your body and keep you vibrant and strong! Why not create a healthy treat to consume through the day? Something that is rich and decadent and guilt-free and has the ability to stave off hunger pains? How about a FAT BOMB? Here's our version of a popular fat bomb that we make all the time. IT'S SO SIMPLE!

PREP TIME: 15–20 minutes
CHILL TIME: 1 hour
MAKES: about 2 dozen fat bombs
SHELF LIFE: 2 weeks in the freezer

1 ¼ cups unsweetened shredded coconut

½ cup raw cashews

½ cup almonds

⅓ cup coconut oil, melted

¼ cup + 1 Tbsp coconut butter

⅓ cup canned full fat coconut milk

¼ cup pumpkin seeds

3 Tbsp cacao nibs

3 medjool dates, pitted

2 Tbsp hemp seeds

1 Tbsp maple syrup

1 tsp cinnamon

1 tsp vanilla extract

½ tsp sea salt

OPTIONAL:
Shredded coconut
Cocoa powder

1. In a food processor, add all of the ingredients and blend until a smooth uniform dough forms. The dough will be somewhat wet, and that's okay.

2. Roll into bite-sized balls, top with optional coconut and/or cocoa, and freeze separately on a baking pan for an hour or so before putting in an airtight container. This way they don't stick together.

TO SERVE: Grab one as your hunger dictates. They're addictive!

Raspberry Cloud Chia Pudding

We love this recipe for a decadent breakfast. But … you could also enjoy it as a light, simple, and easy dessert. This recipe is inspired by a chia seed pudding from Grail Springs, one of our favorite retreat resorts. Located in Northern Ontario, Grail is surrounded by nature and offers equine meditations (yes, horse-led meditations!). It's a truly magical experience. If you can get away for a few days or even a week, and you can't think of where to go, remember Grail Springs in Bancroft, Ontario. Whenever we visit, we leave feeling incredibly grounded and centered. Enjoy this recipe. We promise you will feel like you're on cloud nine.

PREP TIME: 5 minutes
CHILL TIME: 2 hours
MAKES: 4 servings
SHELF LIFE: 2 days in the fridge

2 cups frozen raspberries
¾ cup canned full fat coconut milk
4 Tbsp chia seeds
2 Tbsp maple syrup
1 Tbsp lemon juice

TOPPINGS (PER SERVING):

1 Tbsp fresh raspberries
1 tsp coconut shreds

1. In a blender, blend all of the ingredients until combined and the berry seeds and chia seeds are pulverized (about 2 minutes).

2. Pour the pudding into small dessert cups and refrigerate until cold and set, for a minimum of 2 hours.

3. Top with the raspberries and coconut.

DYK: You can use a blend of frozen strawberries and raspberries for a nice twist. And if you choose to use strawberries, feel free to add fresh strawberries on top!

BREAKFAST | 117

BREAKFAST

Pumpkin Waffles

We love waffles. When Erinn was growing up, Kelly would make these waffles in advance and freeze them so Erinn could pop them in the toaster. They are just like those big brand waffles we can't mention … only these are WAY healthier! They can easily be topped with sliced bananas, peanut butter, berries, local maple syrup, raspberry jam, coconut whipped cream, apple sauce, raw cacao (chocolate) sauce…. You name it! Keep the tradition going with your kids. They will love having something fun, healthy, and yummy for breakfast before school, and they will feel all grown-up toasting it themselves. Of course, you can still enjoy these at any age!

PREP TIME: 10 minutes
COOK TIME: 10–15 minutes
MAKES: 6 medium-sized waffles
SHELF LIFE: 2 days in the fridge or 1 week in the freezer

1½ cups of all-purpose gluten-free flour

½ cup arrowroot starch

1 tsp baking powder

½ tsp baking soda

½ tsp cinnamon

¼ tsp nutmeg

¼ tsp ground ginger

¼ tsp sea salt

1 cup Coconut Milk (page 52)

⅓ cup pumpkin puree

¼ cup melted coconut oil

3 Tbsp maple syrup

2 Tbsp flax meal

2 tsp apple cider vinegar

1 tsp vanilla extract

Coconut oil spray, for greasing (We like Spectrum.)

OPTIONAL TOPPINGS:

Sliced bananas

Peanut butter

Maple syrup

Wild Blueberry Jam (page 111)

Whipped Cream (page 242)

Apple sauce

Cacao Sauce (page 246)

recipe continued

BREAKFAST | 119

1. In a medium bowl, whisk together the flour, arrowroot starch, baking powder, baking soda, cinnamon, nutmeg, ginger, and sea salt.

2. In another medium-size bowl, using a rubber spatula, combine the coconut milk, pumpkin puree, coconut oil, maple syrup, flax meal, apple cider vinegar, and vanilla.

3. Add the dry ingredients to the wet ingredients, and using a hand mixer, mix thoroughly on medium to high speed.

4. Spray your waffle iron with non-stick spray. Heat up your waffle iron over medium heat. Ladle about ½ cup batter (depending on the size of your waffle iron) and slowly close the lid.

5. Cook until slightly browned (about 3 minutes).

TO SERVE: Enjoy right away, or let cool and freeze separately on a baking sheet (so they don't stick together), and then combine in a bag. When ready to re-heat, toast in the toaster, then top with vegan butter, maple syrup, or your favorite topping.

NOTE: This recipe works really well as pancakes too!

BREAKFAST | 121

122 | BREAKFAST

Savory Breakfast Bowl

This savory "porridge" breakfast bowl is one of our favorites and a must when you want some comfort food on a chilly fall day. It's versatile enough to be served for lunch and dinner too. We cook the kale and mushrooms separately, as we find the flavor is better this way. Feel free to sauté them together if you wish to save time.

PREP TIME: 10 minutes
COOK TIME: 15 minutes
MAKES: 2 to 3 servings
SHELF LIFE: 2 days in the fridge

1½ cups vegetable broth

⅓ cup gluten-free rolled oats

⅓ cup red lentils, uncooked

½ tsp garlic powder

½ tsp turmeric

¼ tsp paprika

¼ tsp cumin

¼ tsp sea salt

2–4 soft corn tortillas

1 Tbsp extra-virgin olive oil

1 cup chopped kale

1 cup sliced mushrooms

1 avocado, pitted, peeled, and sliced

1 cup cherry tomatoes, halved

¼ cup Roasted Beet Hummus (page 193) or store-bought classic hummus

1. Preheat the oven to 225°F.

2. In a small saucepan over medium heat, add the vegetable broth, oats, lentils, garlic, turmeric, paprika, cumin, and sea salt. Bring to a boil and then a low simmer. Cook uncovered for 8 to 10 minutes.

3. Wrap the corn tortillas in foil and place them in the oven to warm.

4. Add the olive oil to a frying pan and heat on medium high. Add the mushrooms to the pan and cook until soft (about 5 minutes). Add the kale and sauté until soft and the edges are crispy brown (about 5 minutes).

TO SERVE: Divide the porridge into two bowls. Top with the kale, mushrooms, avocado slices, cherry tomatoes, and a dollop of hummus, with warm tortillas on the side (torn if you wish).

> **DYK:** When you sauté kale, you can remove the bitterness with sea salt. Just a pinch sprinkled on the kale while cooking will do the trick. We love our kale extra browned on the edges for a crisp taste. Yum!

BREAKFAST | 123

Toasts with Avocado

This is our life. Every day, we usually have some form of avocado. Typically, it is on toast, but sometimes we eat it right out of the skin! Hey, when you're hungry, you're hungry! These *three* different avocado-toast variations are great options for different palates and preferences. We promise, you'll love them!

PREP TIME: 5 minutes per variation
MAKES: 2 servings
SHELF LIFE: Serve immediately

TOAST

4 slices gluten-free bread

Drizzle of extra-virgin olive oil

Sea salt, to taste

Desired topping (see variations below)

1. Toast the bread well.

2. Drizzle with olive oil and add a pinch of sea salt.

3. Arrange your desired toppings on the oiled toast.

VARIATION 1: SIMPLE AND DELICIOUS

2 avocados, peeled, pitted, and mashed

1 Tbsp hemp seeds

1 tsp chili flakes

Drizzle of extra-virgin olive oil

Sea salt, to taste

1. Arrange two pieces of toast per plate.

2. Divide the mashed avocado and spread over top the two toasts. Sprinkle each with ½ Tbsp of hemp seeds and ½ tsp of chili flakes, and drizzle with olive oil. Season with sea salt to taste.

recipe continued

BREAKFAST | 125

BREAKFAST

VARIATION 2: HUMMUS AND CHERRY TOMATO

4 Tbsp Beet Hummus (page 193) or store-bought hummus

2 avocados, pitted, peeled, and sliced

½ cup diced cherry tomatoes

1 Tbsp diced fresh basil

Sea salt, to taste

1. Arrange the two pieces of toast per plate.

2. Top each toast with 2 Tbsp of hummus. Then arrange the sliced avocado over the two slices of toast. Add ¼ cup of cherry tomatoes, ½ Tbsp of fresh basil, and sea salt to taste to each piece.

VARIATION 3: HIGH PROTEIN

1 (15 oz) can cannellini beans, rinsed and drained

1 Tbsp lemon juice

2 Tbsp parsley

2 Tbsp basil

1 clove garlic

2 avocados, peeled, pitted, and mashed

Sea salt and pepper, to taste

1. In a heavy-duty blender or food processor, pulse the beans, lemon juice, parsley, basil, and garlic until fully combined, and still somewhat chunky, scraping down the sides as needed.

2. Arrange the two pieces of toast per plate.

3. Divide the mashed avocado and spread over top the two toasts. Then top each with half of the cannellini bean mixture. Add salt and pepper to taste.

DYK: Avocados are loaded with heart-healthy mono-saturated fats.

ALMONDS—
packed with heart-healthy fats.

COCONUT OIL—
contains a unique type of fatty acid called lauric acid, which can help to reduce bad cholesterol levels.

PUMPKIN SEEDS—
are great part of a balanced diet, and they reduce bad cholesterol levels due to alpha-linolenic acid.

WALNUTS — very high in omega-3 fats, which are awesome for your brain!

AVOCADO — can help to reduce bad cholesterol levels. Bring on the avocado toast please!

Fats

Fats are an essential part of our diet to help enhance and maintain cell function, brain health, and keep our hormones functioning optimally.

BRAZIL NUTS — high in heart-healthy fats and high in selenium! Good for men's prostate.

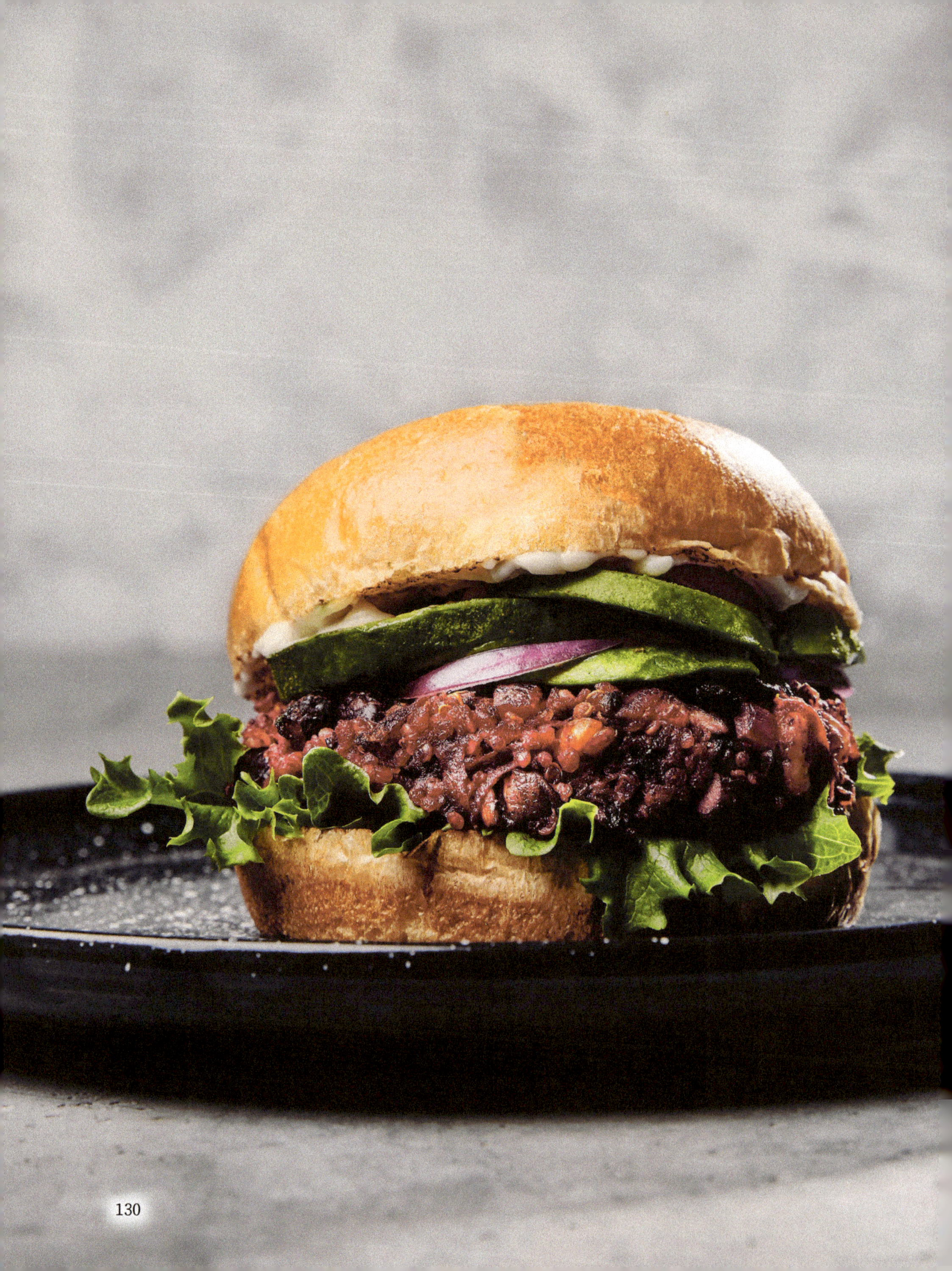

Entrees

Buddha Bowl 2.0   133

Curly Green Bowl   134

Chopped Kale Power Salad   137

Kelp Noodle Salad with Almond Ginger Dressing   138

Loaded Lentil Salad   141

Warm Cauliflower Salad   142

Gut Healing Broth   145

Warming Squash and Carrot Soup   146

Sweet Roasted Corn Soup   149

Triple Goddess Soup   151

Pad Thai   152

Cauliflower Pizza   155

Creamy Polenta with Oven-Roasted Tomatoes, Kale, and Mushrooms   158

Creamy Pumpkin Mac 'n' Cheese   161

Street Beet Burger   162

Sweet Potato Nachos   165

B.L.A.T. Sandwich   166

Cauliflower Steaks with Cashew Butter Kimchi Sauce and Grilled Rapini   169

ENTREES

Buddha Bowl 2.0

The original Buddha Bowl from our first cookbook, *Made With Love,* was the first recipe we made at our first restaurant, Kindfood (now called Lettuce Love Cafe). That's a lot of firsts. We were (and still are) dedicated to creating nutritious and delicious whole foods for everyone. And it worked—that's for sure! Kindfood started it all, and gosh, we respect those days so much. The gratitude and love we received from all our customers and fans was so heartwarming and made us smile all the time! For this book, we decided to re-create our Buddha Bowl and kick it up a notch by enhancing the flavors even more!

PREP TIME: 20 minutes
COOK TIME: 30–45 minutes
MAKES: 4 servings
SHELF LIFE: 4 days in the fridge

2 cups quinoa, rinsed and drained

4 cups vegetable broth

1 tsp extra-virgin olive oil

2 cups greens, sautéed (such as kale, chard, spinach, etc.)

1 cup of Crispy Baked Chickpeas (page 178)

1 cup Turmeric Miso Sauce (page 196)

2 avocados, peeled, pitted, and sliced

4 Tbsp of tamari for garnish

Sesame seeds, for garnish

1. In a medium pot over high heat, add the quinoa and vegetable broth. Cover and bring to a boil. Reduce heat and let simmer for approximately 15 minutes, stirring with a wooden spoon halfway through.

2. In a medium-size frying pan, over medium-high heat, warm the oil. Add the greens. Sauté for 2 to 5 minutes, until soft.

3. Assemble the Buddha Bowl. Start with 1 cup quinoa per bowl. Then top each with ¼ cup of the Crispy Baked Chickpeas, ½ cup of sautéed greens, and ¼ cup of the Turmeric Miso Sauce. Arrange the avocado slices over the top of each bowl, and garnish with sesame seeds.

DYK: We opened our restaurant in 2010, in Downtown Burlington, Ontario, back when being plant-based was not so cool. We proved that when you commit to your passion, and manifest your present reality to support your heart's mission and purpose, you can do anything! Life will open up for you in ways you never dreamt possible.

Curly Green Bowl

This is the perfect summer bowl. It is very fresh tasting and a seasonal treat. This dish is great as leftovers the next day, as the pesto will keep adding flavor to the vegetables. You can serve it as a main dish or a side dish, and even top it with a protein of your choice, such as grilled tempeh or Crispy Baked Chickpeas (page 178)!

PREP TIME: 15 minutes
TOTAL TIME: 30 minutes
MAKES: 4 servings
SHELF LIFE: 2–3 days in the fridge

1 tsp extra-virgin olive oil

Pinch of sea salt

1 head broccoli, diced

4 zucchinis, spiralized

1 cup Pesto (page 190)

½ cup Brazil Nut Parmesan (page 198)

1. In a medium saucepan over medium heat, add the olive oil and a pinch of sea salt and sauté the broccoli until softened (about 5 to 7 minutes).

2. Add the spiralized zucchini to a large bowl. Add the pesto and use tongs to toss well until the zucchini is evenly coated.

TO SERVE: Divide the pasta among 4 pasta bowls. Top each with Brazil Nut parmesan.

DYK: You can buy an inexpensive spiralizer online to use for this recipe. They are easy to use. Please follow the spiralizer instructions.

ENTREES | 135

136 | ENTREES

Chopped Kale Power Salad

This salad is inspired by our first restaurant, Kindfood. The kale in this salad is "massaged" by hand, making it much easier for your body to digest than simply eating raw kale. The more you break down the cellulose fibers, the better for your digestion. Raw kale is really good for your skin. Get that skin glow with this recipe! Note: This salad easily stores in the fridge for future eats.

PREP TIME: 15 minutes
BAKE TIME: 30 minutes
MAKES: 4–6 servings
SHELF LIFE: 4 days in the fridge

2 medium sweet potatoes, peeled

2 tsp + 1 Tbsp extra-virgin olive oil, divided

½ tsp + ¼ tsp sea salt, divided

1 to 2 bunches dinosaur kale, washed, stems removed and chopped (about 7 cups)

½ lemon, juiced

½ cup Lemon Tahini Dressing (page 197)

1 (15 oz) can chickpeas, rinsed and drained

1 avocado, pitted and sliced

⅓ cup dried blueberries

⅓ cup chopped raw almonds

¼ cup red onion, sliced

1. Preheat the oven to 375°F. Line a baking sheet with parchment paper.

2. Cut the sweet potato into uniform slices, and then cut one more time to resemble half-moons. Transfer the sweet potato slices to the prepared baking sheet, drizzle with 2 tsp olive oil and sprinkle with ½ tsp of sea salt. Toss to coat as evenly as possible.

3. Bake the sweet potatoes until fork tender, about 20 to 30 minutes, flipping once halfway through.

4. Meanwhile, in a large bowl, add the chopped kale with 1 Tbsp of olive oil, lemon juice, and ¼ tsp salt. Use your hands to massage the kale. Add the Lemon Tahini Dressing and toss until evenly coated.

TO SERVE: Divide dressed kale among 4 to 6 salad bowls and top each with equal parts sweet potatoes, chickpeas, avocado slices, dried blueberries, almonds, and red onions.

DYK: This salad can be made up in large batches and kept for lunches throughout the week. We recommend keeping the onions out of the salad if you're going to keep it for leftovers, as the onion flavor will overpower every other vegetable in the salad ... and your fridge!

Kelp Noodle Salad with Almond Ginger Dressing

Who knew you could make noodles from kelp?! We first fell in love with kelp noodles during our early days at our first restaurant, Kindfood, and so did our customers! Kelp noodles are very high in iodine and are low carb too, making them a great healthy addition to your menu. Erinn says it is one of her favorite salads—she loves the freshness and the CRUNCH.

PREP TIME: 15 minutes
MAKES: 4 servings
SHELF LIFE: 3 days in the fridge

8 cups kelp noodles

½ cup chopped mint

½ cup chopped cilantro

½ cup Almond Ginger Dressing (page 196)

1 avocado, pitted, peeled, and thinly sliced

2 Tbsp black sesame seeds

¼ cup crushed raw organic peanuts or raw organic almonds

Hot sauce, to taste (optional)

1. In a large bowl, combine the kelp noodles, mint, and cilantro. Add the Almond Ginger Dressing, and toss to coat. Add more dressing if you'd like your noodles to be a little saucier.

TO SERVE: Portion the salad into four bowls. Top with avocado, black sesame seeds, nuts, and optional hot sauce. Enjoy the crunch of the kelp noodles!

DYK: You can find kelp noodles at your local health-food store in the refrigerated section.

ENTREES | 139

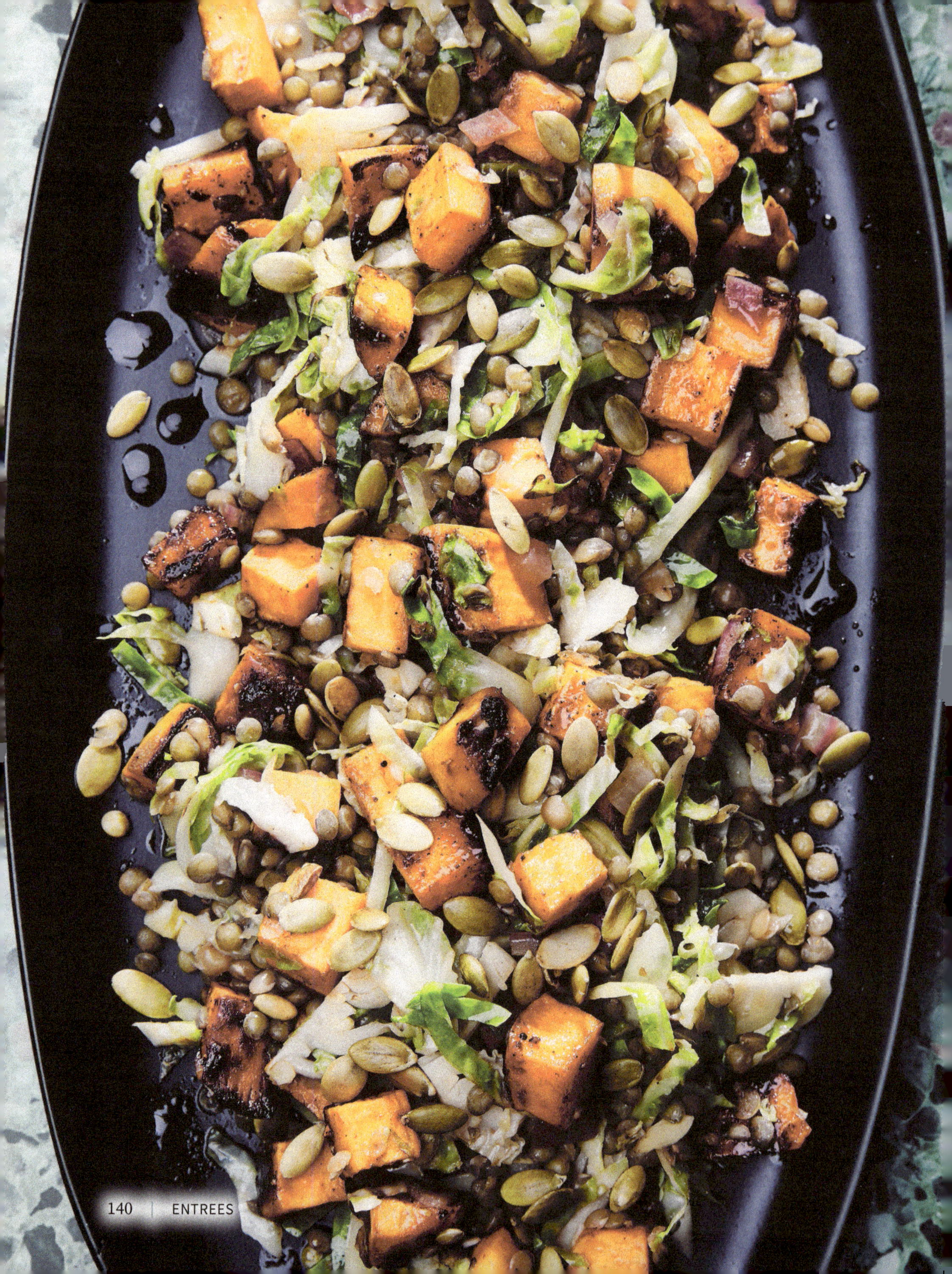

Loaded Lentil Salad

Lentils are one of our favorite protein sources. This entree is loaded with healthy stuff! We love the added flavors and textures that the roasted brussels sprouts (YUM!), spiced-up sweet potato, and toasted pumpkin seeds add to this recipe. We love our brussels sprouts braised up dark brown. We could eat bowlfuls of them! We love it all!

PREP TIME: 15 minutes
COOK TIME: 30 minutes
MAKES: 2–4 servings
SHELF LIFE: 2 days in the fridge

2 Tbsp extra virgin olive oil, divided
1 red onion, diced
1 cup French lentils, rinsed and drained
3 cups filtered water
2 tsp balsamic vinegar
2 pinches sea salt
2 medium sweet potatoes, peeled and diced into ½ inch cubes
½ tsp chili pepper
½ tsp cumin
2 tsp maple syrup
2 cups brussels sprouts, thinly sliced
⅓ cup pumpkin seeds, toasted
Sea salt and pepper, to taste

1. Preheat the oven to 425°F. Line a baking sheet with parchment paper.

2. In a medium saucepan over medium heat, warm 1 tsp of olive oil. Add the red onions and cook until softened, about 5 minutes. Add the lentils and filtered water. Bring to a boil and then lower the heat and simmer, uncovered, until tender (about 15 to 20 minutes). Drain any excess water from cooking the lentils. Return to pot. Add balsamic vinegar and pinch of sea salt and stir.

3. In a medium bowl, combine the sweet potatoes, chili pepper, cumin, maple syrup, 1 Tbsp of olive oil, and a pinch of sea salt. Arrange the sweet-potato mixture in a single layer onto the prepared baking sheet, and bake until golden brown, about 10 minutes per side, tossing halfway through. Remove and place in a bowl.

4. In an iron skillet over medium heat, warm 2 tsp of olive oil and a pinch of sea salt. Add the brussels sprouts and cook until golden brown, about 8 to 10 minutes.

5. Add the pumpkin seeds to the prepared baking sheet and toast for 5 minutes.

TO SERVE: Plate the lentils in two to four bowls and top each with sweet potato mixture, brussels sprouts, toasted pumpkin seeds, and salt and pepper to taste.

Warm Cauliflower Salad

When we crave vegetables in the winter, we change up our salads with heartier vegetables and ingredients that have warm flavors like roasted cauliflower and smoked paprika. This salad, perfect for winter, keeps well in the fridge, making it great for on-the-go lunches.

PREP TIME: 10 minutes
COOK TIME: 15 minutes
MAKES: 2–4 servings
SHELF LIFE: 2–3 days in fridge

2 Tbsp extra-virgin olive oil

1 head cauliflower, diced

½ tsp smoked paprika

2 cups fresh baby spinach

1 cup Crispy Baked Chickpeas (page 178)

½ cup Lemon Tahini Dressing (page 197), or Turmeric Miso Sauce (page 196)

Lemon wedges, for serving

Sea salt and ground pepper, to taste

1. In a medium saucepan, over medium heat, heat the olive oil. Add the cauliflower and paprika, and sauté until the edges of the cauliflower are slightly browned (about 7 minutes).

2. Add the spinach, and the Crispy Baked Chickpeas, stirring until the spinach is slightly wilted (about 3 to 5 minutes).

3. Serve tossed with Lemon Tahini Dressing or Turmeric Miso Sauce and lemon wedges on the side. Salt and pepper to taste.

ENTREES | 143

144 | ENTREES

Gut Healing Broth

There are so many incredible health benefits to broths, and a lot of talk recently about bone broth to help with gut health. We developed this recipe as a plant-based version to help give your immune system and digestive tract all of the nutrients it needs to heal and keep you healthy and strong, especially during the winter months. Make a lot of it and store in your freezer, so it's ready to go. Simply defrost, heat, and serve. Note: This can be consumed for breakfast. Just saying....

PREP TIME: 20 minutes
COOK TIME: 1 hour, 10 minutes
MAKES: 10–12 servings
SHELF LIFE: 1 week in the fridge or up to 3 months in the freezer

12 cups filtered water

4 cups of roughly chopped vegetables of your choice (we like celery, leeks, carrots, cabbage)

1 cup roughly chopped greens (we like kale or spinach)

1 cup shiitake mushrooms

1 cup cremini mushrooms

¼ cup nutritional yeast

2 Tbsp wakame seaweed

2 Tbsp turmeric powder

4 Tbsp brown miso paste

1 Tbsp extra-virgin olive oil

1 red onion, quartered, with skins

1 garlic bulb, smashed and peeled

1 small chili pepper with seeds

1 (3-inch) knob ginger, peeled and roughly chopped

1 tsp peppercorn

1 tsp sea salt

1 bunch fresh basil or cilantro

1. Add all of the ingredients to a large pot. Bring to a boil and then cover and simmer for an hour or more. Strain.

TO SERVE: Enjoy immediately if you wish or refrigerate or freeze for a later date.

> **DYK:** If you choose to keep any of the vegetables after straining, we choose the mushrooms. We don't like to waste anything. Add them to a salad or to top off a rice bowl. They are a superfood and have immense gut-healing and immunity-boosting properties. They have been known to help fight off illnesses, especially during the colder, darker winter months. If you don't have use for them in a recipe, you can use them as compost for your garden!

Warming Squash and Carrot Soup

Soup is a mainstay in our fridges, and I think it's because you can effortlessly get all kinds of nutrition from it. There's nothing like curling up in front of the fireplace, grabbing a great book to read, and indulging in a mug of soup to warm you to the bone. This soup in particular has a beautiful, deep, rich taste that will definitely warm you up on those cooler fall and winter days.

PREP TIME: 10 minutes
COOK TIME: 30 minutes
MAKES: 8–10 servings
SHELF LIFE: 4 days in the fridge or 2 months in the freezer

2 Tbsp coconut oil

1 butternut squash, peeled, seeded, and cut into ½-inch pieces

2 carrots, diced

1 yellow onion, diced

4 cloves garlic, chopped

2 Tbsp Thai red curry paste

2 tsp red pepper flakes

1 tsp ground coriander

1 tsp ground cumin

½ tsp sea salt

4 cups vegetable broth

1 cup canned coconut milk, plus extra for garnish

2 Tbsp fresh lime juice

Zest of 1 lime

Cilantro, for garnish

1. Heat coconut oil in a large pot over medium heat. Add the squash, carrots, onion, garlic, red curry paste, red pepper flakes, coriander, cumin, and sea salt.

2. Cook, stirring occasionally until onion is translucent (about 8 to 10 minutes). Add the broth, bring mixture to a boil, and then reduce heat to a simmer until squash is soft (about 15 to 20 minutes).

3. Taste, and add a little more red pepper flakes and/or red curry paste if it's not spicy enough for you.

4. Add the coconut milk and stir. Cook the soup for another 4 to 5 minutes to deepen the flavor. Add the lime juice and zest.

5. Slowly, add a little soup at a time to a heavy-duty blender. Blend until smooth, and transfer into a large bowl.

TO SERVE: Season to taste, and ladle into individual bowls. Garnish with coconut milk and cilantro. If you want to go another step try toasted shredded coconut as a garnish. It is divine.

ENTREES | 147

148 | ENTREES

Sweet Roasted Corn Soup

Kelly posted this soup recipe to her blog in 2012, and the response was incredible! Every year since, it gets re-posted during the summer corn-harvest months to many happy fans. Whip this simple vegan recipe up for an easy dinner, and we bet you that there will be no leftovers.

PREP TIME: 15 minutes
COOK TIME: 20 minutes
MAKES: 6-8 servings
SHELF LIFE: 4 days in the fridge or 2 months in the freezer

1 Tbsp extra-virgin olive oil
2 medium yellow onions, finely diced
3 stalks celery, diced
2 cloves garlic, peeled and minced
½ tsp dried chili flakes
5 +1 cups corn kernels (make sure they're non-gmo and organic!)
¼ cup vegan butter
4 cups vegetable broth
2 Tbsp diced sundried tomatoes
1 Tbsp maple syrup
½ cup canned coconut milk
Sea salt, to taste

GARNISH:

Sundried tomatoes
Parsley
Chili flakes
Fresh ground pepper

1. In a large pot over medium heat, warm the olive oil. Add the onions and sauté for 1 minute. Add the celery, garlic, and chili flakes, and continue to sauté until onions are soft and translucent (about 3 to 4 minutes).

2. In an iron skillet over medium-high heat, add the corn and butter and cook until browned (about 5 to 7 minutes).

3. In the large pot, add the broth, sundried tomatoes, and maple syrup. Bring to a simmer and cook for 10 minutes until soup has reduced slightly and thickened.

4. Add the coconut milk and stir. Remove from heat. In a heavy-duty blender, blend the soup in batches. Add remaining corn. Salt to taste.

TO SERVE: Portion out into 6+ bowls, and top each with your choice of fresh parsley, sundried tomatoes, chili flakes and ground pepper.

ENTREES | 149

ENTREES

Triple Goddess Soup

Embrace your inner goddess with this delicious soup filled with veggie goodness. This is the second recipe in this book inspired by one of our favorite retreats: Grail Springs Retreat Centre. Gosh, we love that place so much! We hope you love this recipe as much as we do. And trust us, there is a lot of soup here to last you through the week or to share with friends. We have been known to eat this for breakfast or put it in a travel mug to ensure we are getting fortified the way we need to. It's the perfect way to get lots of greens for the day.

PREP TIME: 10 minutes
COOK TIME: 25 minutes
MAKES: 6–8 hearty servings
SHELF LIFE: 5 days in the fridge or 1 month in the freezer

1 Tbsp extra-virgin olive oil
1 medium onion, chopped
½ tsp chili flakes
2 stalks celery, chopped
1 medium head of broccoli, chopped
4 cups vegetable broth
2 cups baby spinach
¾ cup sweet peas, fresh or frozen
½ cup fresh basil
¼ tsp sea salt or to taste
Pinch of pepper
Bread, for serving

1. In a large pot over medium heat, sauté the onions and chili flakes in olive oil until translucent (about 4 minutes).

2. Add the celery and broccoli, and sauté until celery starts to soften (about 5 minutes).

3. Add the vegetable broth and stir. Bring to a boil. Reduce the heat and simmer until the vegetables are soft, about 10 minutes. In the last 5 minutes of cooking, add the spinach, peas, basil, and salt. Continue cooking until all vegetables are cooked through and softened.

4. Transfer soup to a heavy-duty blender. Blend in small batches until smooth.

5. Season with salt and pepper to taste.

TO SERVE: Ladle into large soup bowls and garnish with fresh basil. Serve with a large crusty piece of bread. YES!

Pad Thai

Ahhhhh, beautiful Thailand.... After experiencing all of the wonderful food there, we were inspired to recreate our favorite dish when we got back home: Pad Thai. This dish is versatile and easy with a plant-based twist!

PREP TIME: 20 minutes
COOK TIME: 25 minutes
MAKES: 4 servings
SHELF LIFE: 4–5 days in the fridge

½ cup wheat-free tamari

1 cup organic carrot juice (store bought if in a pinch)

¼ cup + 3 Tbsp organic peanut butter

¼ cup + 1 Tbsp lime juice

1 Tbsp ginger

½ tsp dried chili flakes

2 (250 g) packages of sweet potato and buckwheat noodles or Thai rice noodles

1 tsp extra-virgin olive oil

Pinch of sea salt

4 cups kale, remove stalks and tear into pieces

2 large carrots, shredded

½ cup cashews, coarsely chopped

Handful of bean sprouts

1. In a heavy-duty blender, blend the tamari, carrot juice, peanut butter, lime juice, ginger, and chili flakes until combined and smooth. If too thick, add a Tbsp more of carrot juice.

2. In a large pot over medium-high heat, cook pasta according to the package instructions.

3. While the pasta is cooking, heat a large iron skillet with olive oil and lightly sprinkle with sea salt. Add the kale and sauté for approximately 5 minutes until softened. Add the carrots and cook for about 2 to 3 minutes. Remove from the heat.

4. Drain the pasta well and put into frying pan with kale and carrots. Gently stir. Add the sauce, and gently stir to combine.

TO SERVE: Using tongs or a pasta scoop, divide equally among the 4 bowls and top each with chopped cashews and bean sprouts. To reheat the Pad Thai, turn heat to low, splash with a little filtered water, and cover for 3–5 minutes.

DYK: Thailand is one of our favorite places in the world. It's where Erinn spent some time at the Elephant Nature Park sanctuary, helped build elephant habitats, and learned all about these beautiful creatures. Sweet bliss.

Our photo includes tempeh and wanting to keep this recipe as quick and simple as possible, we decided to make the tempeh an 'add-on'. We cut 1 - 8 ounce package of tempeh into ½" cubes and marinate in tamari sauce for 30 minutes, then toss the tempeh into the frying pan and cook for 10 minutes. Then continue the recipe by adding kale and carrots.

154 | ENTREES

Cauliflower Pizza

Looking for a grain-free pizza crust? This cauliflower crust boasts a great alternative to the high-carb and excessive bloating version of white flour. We seriously love cauliflower pizza! Question! Do you like pineapple on pizza?! Erinn does, and Kelly doesn't! So, please top it as you would your favorite pizza!

NOTE: We pre-cook the veggie toppings so that the moisture will not end up in the cauliflower crust while they are cooking. The goal here is to have a crispy cauliflower crust and not a soggy one that falls apart.

PREP TIME: 25 minutes
COOK/ASSEMBLY TIME: 1 hour
MAKES: 3-4 appetizer servings
SHELF LIFE: 2 days in the fridge

1 Tbsp cornmeal
6 cups cauliflower florets or 1 large head of cauliflower
2 Tbsp flaxseed meal
¼ cup nutritional yeast
3 cloves minced garlic
1 tsp red pepper flakes
½ tsp oregano
½ tsp dried basil
¼ tsp sea salt
3 Tbsp arrowroot starch (use cornstarch as a substitute)
1 cup mushrooms, sliced
1 cup spinach
½ bell pepper, chopped
¼ cup pineapple (optional, will add more moisture to pizza so be careful!)
½ cup store-bought marinara sauce

SUGGESTED TOPPINGS:
Fresh basil
Nutritional yeast

1. Preheat the oven to 395°F. Line a perforated baking sheet with parchment paper. Sprinkle with a little cornmeal. Set aside.

2. Cut the cauliflower into florets. Using a grater or a food processor, grate or pulse florets to create small rice-sized pieces. Set aside.

3. Bring a large pot of water to a boil. Add the cauliflower. Cook for 4 minutes to soften. Drain the cauliflower in a fine mesh strainer. Let cool.

4. Use a clean dish towel or paper towel (or even a cheese cloth) to remove as much excess liquid as possible. This step is very important as you don't want the crust to be wet.

5. In a small bowl, combine the flaxseed meal and 3 Tbsp of water. Let sit for 5 minutes to thicken.

recipe continued

ENTREES | 155

6. In a large mixing bowl, add the cauliflower rice, nutritional yeast, garlic, red pepper flakes, oregano, basil, sea salt, and arrowroot starch. Then add the flax egg and stir with a mixing spoon or your hands to thoroughly combine. A loose dough should form. Taste and adjust flavor as needed, adding more nutritional yeast for a cheesy flavor. If the dough is too wet, add a little more arrowroot starch, and if it's too dry, add a little water.

7. Using your hands, spread the dough onto the prepared parchment and flatten the crust until it is slightly less than ½ inch thick.

8. Bake the crust for 45 minutes, then remove and flip the crust to bake on the other side for another 10 minutes.

9. Meanwhile, in a medium frying pan over medium heat, cook the mushrooms, spinach, peppers, and pineapple until slightly tender, but not too soft. It's important to cook the toppings beforehand to prevent them from making the crust soggy while baking.

10. Remove the pizza from the oven and top with the marinara and vegetable toppings, fresh basil, and nutritional yeast. Bake for another 10–15 minutes until toppings are tender. Watch the edges of the crust, which can get brown before the toppings.

TO SERVE: Enjoy HOT with additional toppings if needed. Store any leftovers in the fridge for up to 2 days.

NOTE: To save some time with this recipe, you can purchase pre-riced cauliflower at many grocery stores!

ENTREES | 157

Creamy Polenta with Oven-Roasted Tomatoes, Kale, and Mushrooms

This recipe has been a staple in our homes for years. It's very simple to make, and it will impress your guests! The goal with this recipe is to create a soft, pourable polenta and not a clumping one. You'll love it!

PREP TIME: 15 minutes
COOK AND BAKE TIME: 1 hour
MAKES: 2 servings
SHELF LIFE: 4 days in the fridge

2 cups Roasted Tomatoes (page 189)

4 cups vegetable broth

1⅓ cup cornmeal

1 tsp finely diced fresh sage

1 tsp finely diced fresh rosemary

¼ tsp sea salt

2 tsp extra-virgin olive oil

2 cups sliced cremini mushrooms

1 large bunch of kale, de-stemmed and torn into bite-sized pieces

Drizzle of store-bought balsamic reduction (optional)

1. In a medium saucepan, add the vegetable broth and bring to a slight boil. Add the cornmeal, sage, rosemary, and ¼ tsp of salt, gradually, and stir until fully incorporated. Reduce heat, cover and cook for about 30 minutes, whisking every 3–5 minutes until the polenta is creamy in texture and the individual grains are tender. If the polenta gets too thick to whisk while cooking, add some water or more veggie broth. Set aside.

2. In a medium-sized frying pan over medium heat, add 1 tsp of olive oil. Add the mushrooms and sauté for 5 to 7 minutes or until mushrooms are golden. Remove and set aside.

3. In the same pan, add the kale and remaining olive oil and sauté until kale is cooked and softened (about 5 minutes).

TO SERVE: Scoop the polenta equally into 2 pasta bowls. Then top each with roasted tomatoes, mushrooms, and kale. Drizzle with balsamic reduction.

ENTREES | 159

ENTREES

Creamy Pumpkin Mac 'n' Cheese

Perfect for a cozy fall or winter day. Pumpkin is such a great way to swap out the cheese, giving the mac 'n' cheese an amazing richness and creaminess. We think this photo says it all. This is an incredible dish for the Thanksgiving season, and trust us, your guests will not forget this dish. You might want to double the sauce and have more for alternate uses like a pumpkin sauce for mashed potatoes or broccoli. YUM!

PREP TIME: 10 minutes
COOK TIME: 30 minutes
MAKES: 4 servings
SHELF LIFE: 2–3 days in the fridge

1 (12 oz) package gluten-free macaroni noodles (see note)

2 cups of organic, canned pumpkin puree

1 cup Coconut Milk (page 52) or store-bought unsweetened coconut milk

⅓ cup nutritional yeast

1 large clove garlic (or 2 small cloves)

2 Tbsp arrowroot starch

1 tsp chopped fresh thyme

1 Tbsp chopped fresh sage

¼ tsp pumpkin pie spice

½ tsp red pepper flakes

½ tsp sea salt, and more to taste

1. In a large pot over medium-high heat, cook pasta according to the package instructions. Drain and set aside.

2. In a blender, combine the pumpkin puree, coconut milk, nutritional yeast, garlic, arrowroot starch, thyme, sage, pumpkin pie spice, red pepper flakes, and sea salt until smooth. Add to a large saucepan over medium heat, whisking frequently until the sauce is hot and slightly thickened (about 5 minutes). If the sauce becomes too thick, add some more coconut milk.

3. Add the cooked pasta to the saucepan and toss to combine. Serve as is, or transfer to an open casserole dish and put under the broiler until lightly browned (about 2 to 3 minutes).

TO SERVE: Enjoy hot. Pairs well with cozying up on your couch with your favorite show on Netflix.

NOTE: We like to use quinoa, brown rice, or chickpea pastas. We have found that they are the best-cooking gluten-free options on the market.

Street Beet Burger

While Erinn was away on the beautiful island of Kauai, she found this incredible burger place. They had a smoked *beet* burger on their menu that was to die for. Yes! BEET! Not beef! This recipe is inspired by Erinn's exceptional and incredible beet-burger experience. Choose your favorite bun from sourdough to gluten-free to multi-grain…. The list is endless. You can also go "bun-less" and wrap your burger in romaine lettuce leaves. Easy, right?

PREP TIME: 15 minutes
COOK TIME: 10 minutes
CHILL TIME: 1 hour
MAKES: 6 patties or 10 to 12 sliders
SHELF LIFE: 4 days in the fridge, or frozen for up to 1 month

1 Tbsp chia seeds

1 Tbsp flaxseed meal

1 tsp extra-virgin olive oil

½ cup diced red onion

1 cup finely diced cremini mushrooms

1 (15 oz) can of black beans, rinsed and drained

1 cup finely grated raw beet

1 cup white quinoa, cooked

¾ cup chopped raw walnuts

1 tsp chili powder

1 tsp ground cumin

1 tsp smoked paprika

1 tsp sea salt

OPTIONAL TOPPINGS:

2 avocados, pitted, peeled, and sliced

1 tomato, sliced

Lettuce

Vegan Mayo (page 197)

Burger or slider buns, for serving

1. In a small bowl, combine the chia seeds with 3 Tbsp of water. In another small bowl, combine the flaxseed meal with 3 Tbsp of water. Set aside.

2. In a medium saucepan over medium heat, add the olive oil, red onion, and cremini mushrooms. Sauté until the vegetables are soft and fragrant (about 5 minutes).

3. Add the black beans to the mushroom mixture, and using a masher (or a fork), pulverize the beans until they are almost all mashed. (You'll want a little bit of texture left.)

4. Transfer the mushroom and bean mixture to a large mixing bowl and add the beets, cooked quinoa, walnuts, chili powder, cumin, paprika, and sea salt. Stir well to combine.

recipe continued

5. Add the chia mixture and flax mixture, and mix well (by hand, if needed).

6. Form the burgers into about 6 patties, or 10 to 12 sliders, and refrigerate for 1 hour to firm up.

7. Meanwhile, preheat the BBQ to medium heat.

8. Once burgers are firmed up, grill them on the barbecue or an oiled frying pan for 6 to 7 minutes on each side.

TO SERVE: Place the burger on a bun of your choice, and garnish with your choice of toppings such as lettuce, avocado, tomato, mayo, mustard, etc. Enjoy!

164 | ENTREES

Sweet Potato Nachos

Nachos appeal to pretty much everyone and are a favorite for sure. We wanted to showcase how healthy and versatile vegetables can be! This recipe does just that. Open your heart, mind, and soul to the possibility that this recipe could make you give up animal-based foods for one meal. Let's start here.

PREP TIME: 20 minutes
BAKE AND COOK TIME: 1 hour
MAKES: 4 servings
SHELF LIFE: 2 days in the fridge

4 large sweet potatoes, thinly sliced lengthwise (or use a mandolin for a very thin slice!)

1 cup organic, store-bought barbecue sauce

1 can (19 oz) jackfruit in water, drained

1 cup filtered water

1 cup Easy Cheese Sauce (page 194)

SUGGESTED TOPPINGS:

1 avocado, peeled and diced

2 ears of corn, grilled and cut from the cob

1 tomato, diced in ½-inch pieces

Jalapeno, sliced and seeds removed

Red onion, peeled and diced

Lime wedges

Favorite store-bought salsa

Guacamole (page 181)

Sliced radishes (optional)

1. Preheat the oven to 375°F. Line a baking sheet with parchment paper. Place the sliced sweet potatoes on the sheet, and bake for approximately 20–30 minutes, or until soft.

2. Increase the heat to 450°F and cook for an additional 5–10 minutes, until golden and crispy. Keep the oven on at 400°F. Remove from oven.

3. While the sweet potatoes are baking, in a medium saucepan over medium heat, add the barbecue sauce, jackfruit, and water. Cook until the liquid is reduced by half (20–30 minutes).

4. Replace the parchment paper on the baking sheet with new clean parchment paper. Pile on the sweet potatoes and top with barbequed jackfruit. Bake for 10 minutes at 400°F.

5. Remove from the oven, and top with a drizzle of Easy Cheese Sauce.

6. Top with avocado, corn, tomato, jalapeno, red onion, lime wedges, salsa, and guac. Adios amigo!

DYK: Jackfruit is known as a plant-based (vegan) replacement for "pulled pork."

ENTREES | 165

The B.L.A.T. Sandwich

Bac'un, lettuce, avocado, and tomato from our original Kindfood cafe in 2010—often imitated, never duplicated. This sandwich may sound very simple to create, but the final resulting taste is all in the quality of its ingredients. Enjoy this sandwich, while we walk down memory lane.

PREP TIME: 5 minutes
MAKES: 2 servings
SHELF LIFE: Good until lunchtime!

4 pieces of gluten-free bread, toasted
4 Tbsp The Best Vegan Mayo (page 197)
1 avocado, peeled and sliced
1 tomato, sliced
2 pieces of romaine lettuce
8 strips of Carrot Bacon (page 174)
Pinch of sea salt

1. Toast your 4 slices of bread.

2. Spread a generous serving of vegan mayo on each slice of toasted bread and place on a plate face up.

3. Layer your sandwich, starting with avocado and tomato.

4. Then sprinkle the tomato with a small amount of salt.

5. Add romaine and then Carrot Bacon.

6. Add a small amount of Vegan Mayo to the other two slices of toast.

7. Place the second piece of bread (toast) on top of each of your sandwiches, and slice on a diagonal.

8. Enjoy! We told you it's easy. Don't forget the most important ingredient, LOVE!

ENTREES | 167

168 | ENTREES

Cauliflower Steaks with Cashew Butter Kimchi Sauce and Grilled Rapini

Sigh! The thought of enjoying this meal in Prince Edward County brings us such joy. This recipe in particular was created with inspiration from Flame and Smith restaurant and Chef Hidde. Thank you! Their version was with a brown-butter kimchi sauce as an accompaniment to their fire-roasted cauliflower steak.

PREP TIME: 20 minutes
COOK TIME: 45 minutes
MAKES: 4–6 servings
SHELF LIFE: 4 days in fridge

CAULIFLOWER STEAKS:

2 large heads cauliflower, cut 1-inch thick

2 Tbsp extra-virgin olive oil

2 lemons, zested and juiced

2 cloves garlic, finely minced

1 tsp sea salt

¼ tsp red pepper flakes

1 cup raw cashews roasted or grilled with cauliflower steaks

1. Remove the outer leaves from each cauliflower head. Cut off the bottom stem end so that you create a flat base and can stand the cauliflower up on a cutting board. Resting the cauliflower on the stem, use a large, sharp knife to trim away the sides, then cut the remaining head into 4 very thick or 6 more moderate "steaks," each 1-inch thick.

2. Heat broiler to medium heat in oven. Or use GRILL and heat to 350°F.

3. If using BROILER: Lay steaks on top of broiler pan. Brush one side of each cauliflower steak with the lemon, garlic, and olive oil mixture, and then sprinkle the brushed sides with half of the salt. Flip over and repeat. Ensure the cauliflower is browning for 5 minutes before flipping over to the other side (5–6 minutes each side total time).

recipe continued

4. If using GRILL: Lay steaks on grill and brush with lemon, olive oil, and garlic, then sprinkle with salt. Flip over and repeat. Cover the grill and let cook for 5 to 6 minutes until the bottom is beginning to char. Flip the cauliflower, then re-cover the grill, and cook 5 additional minutes, until the cauliflower is tender. Remove from the grill. Sprinkle with the red pepper flakes.

5. Place 1 cup of roasted cashews on small cookie sheet or oven-safe pan to brown or toss on grill with cauliflower steaks. Let brown too.

KIMCHI CASHEW BUTTER SAUCE:

1 cup raw cashews

1½ cups filtered water

1 tsp tamari

2 tsp sesame oil

1 Tbsp tahini

½ cup kimchi, broiled for 3-5 minutes

1. Add all ingredients to a heavy-duty blender and blend until smooth. About 1–2 minutes.

GRILLED RAPINI

1 bunch rapini (broccoli rabe), trimmed and cut into pieces (or 1 broccoli cut into florets)

1 Tbsp extra-virgin olive oil

1 clove garlic, chopped

Sea salt and pepper

1. In a saucepan of salted boiling water, blanch rapini for 2 to 3 minutes or until *al dente*. Cool quickly under cold water. Drain.

2. In a large skillet, add olive oil and brown the garlic and blanched rapini over medium heat for 3 to 5 minutes.

3. Add a touch of sea salt and pepper and serve.

ENTREES | 171

172

Sauces, Sides, and Snacks

Carrot Bacon   174

Eazy Cheezy Kale Chips   177

Crispy Baked Chickpeas   178

Guac and Chips   181

Movie Night Popcorn   182

Friday Night Dip   185

Quick and Easy Pickled Vegetables   186

Oven-Roasted Tomatoes   189

Classic Pesto   190

Roasted Beet Hummus   193

Easy Cheese Sauce   194

Turmeric Miso Sauce   196

Almond Ginger Dressing   196

The Best Vegan Mayo   197

Lemon Tahini Dressing   197

Our Famous Brazil Nut Parmesan   198

Carrot Bacon

We love this carrot bacon. It's so easy to make and the perfect addition to your B.L.A.T. Sandwich! (page 166) Your kids will also love Carrot Bacon as an after school snack or in their lunches.

PREP TIME: 5 minutes
BAKE TIME: 20 minutes
MAKES: about 12 slices of bacon (depending on size of carrots)
SHELF LIFE: 5 days in the fridge, preferably uncovered

2 large carrots
1–2 tsp coconut oil
¼ tsp sweet paprika
¼ tsp chili powder
Sea salt, to taste

1. Preheat the oven to 350°F. Line a baking sheet with parchment paper.

2. Using a vegetable peeler, make long thin ribbons with the carrots.

3. In a small bowl, combine the coconut oil, paprika, chili powder, and sea salt.

4. Add the carrots and mix until they are evenly coated, making sure the carrots aren't drenched in oil.

5. Place the strips in a single layer on the prepared baking sheet. Do not let them overlap.

6. Bake until slightly golden, about 20 minutes.

TO SERVE: Use as you would bacon.

SAUCES, SIDES, AND SNACKS | 175

176 | SAUCES, SIDES, AND SNACKS

Eazy Cheezy Kale Chips

Kale chips have always seemed so daunting to us. Most vegan raw-food kale-chip recipes call for a dehydrator and can take upwards of twenty-four hours to make! I don't know about you, but who has that kind of time? Or that kind of space in their home? We've created a recipe that's quick and easy and still full of the nutrient goodness from kale!

PREP TIME: 5 minutes
BAKE TIME: 20 minutes
MAKES: 4 cups
SHELF LIFE: 1 week at room temperature

6 cups kale, destemmed, torn into pieces
3 Tbsp extra-virgin olive oil
¼ cup raw cashews
3 Tbsp sunflower seeds
⅓ cup nutritional yeast
½ tsp sea salt
¼ tsp black pepper
Pinch cayenne pepper (optional)

DYK: Nutritional yeast isn't actually a yeast; it's a mold (sounds gross and weird, but it's a healthy mold) that grows on molasses. It gives vegan food a nice cheesy flavor! It is high in vitamin B12 too!

1. Preheat the oven to 250°F. Line a baking sheet with parchment paper.

2. In a large mixing bowl, add the kale and drizzle with the olive oil. Using your hands, massage the kale to coat with oil and soften the leaves.

3. In a heavy-duty blender on high speed, or small food processor, pulse the cashews, sunflower seeds, nutritional yeast, sea salt, pepper, and cayenne into a fine powder. You may need to scrape down the sides with a spatula as needed.

4. Add the processed nut mixture to the kale and toss to combine, making sure all of the kale leaves are evenly coated.

5. Arrange the kale in a single layer on the prepared baking sheet.

6. Bake for 15 minutes, then toss to ensure even baking. Bake until slightly crispy, another 5 to 10 minutes.

Crispy Baked Chickpeas

Add these crispy baked chickpeas to your favorite salad, on top of Avocado Toast (page 124), or just snack on them on their own. They're packed with protein and fiber too.

PREP TIME: 5 minutes
BAKE TIME: 35 minutes
MAKES: 1 cup
SHELF LIFE: 1 week at room temperature

1 can (15 oz) of chickpeas
1 Tbsp extra-virgin olive oil
½ tsp sea salt

1. Preheat the oven to 350°F. Line a baking sheet with parchment paper.

2. Drain and rinse the chickpeas. Spread the chickpeas out on an absorbent towel and use your hands to gently roll and thoroughly dry the chickpeas.

3. Transfer the chickpeas to a mixing bowl and top with oil and salt. Stir evenly to coat.

4. Place chickpeas on a parchment lined baking sheet. Bake for 30 minutes. Using oven mitts, shake the pan and then rotate to allow for even cooking. Cook for an additional 5 minutes.

5. Remove from oven.

TO SERVE: Toss with additional seasonings or salt if desired, let cool for 5 minutes before eating.

SAUCES, SIDES, AND SNACKS | 179

180 | SAUCES, SIDES, AND SNACKS

Guac and Chips

This is one of our favorite recipes for a reason. Guacamole is a staple in both of our households, mostly because it's a great excuse to eat more avocados (not that we need one).

PREP TIME: 10 minutes
MAKES: 4 servings
SHELF LIFE: 1 day in the fridge

3 avocados, peeled and pitted
1 cup halved cherry tomatoes
1 Tbsp minced red onion
3 Tbsp lime juice
½ tsp sea salt, to taste
2 Tbsp chopped cilantro
1 jalapeño, seeds removed, diced
1 bag of corn tortilla chips

1. In a medium mixing bowl, mash the avocados. Add the cherry tomatoes, red onions, lime juice, sea salt, cilantro, and jalapeño, and mix until combined.

TO SERVE: Enjoy immediately or refrigerate for 30 minutes to let the flavors marry. Serve with corn tortillas or eat it right out of the bowl with a spoon!

Movie Night Popcorn

When you want to stay home and watch a movie, why not make some healthier popcorn?! In this recipe, we've given you the option to either use non-GMO popcorn kernels or cauliflower for those of you sensitive to corn. Once Erinn gets started, it's hard for her to stop eating this delicious popcorn!

PREP TIME: 10 minutes
COOK & BAKE TIME: 15-30 minutes
MAKES: 3–4 to servings
SHELF LIFE: 1 week at room temperature for popcorn and in the fridge for cauliflower

1 cup non-GMO popcorn kernels
¼ cup melted coconut oil, divided
¼ cup nutritional yeast
½ tsp paprika
½ tsp chipotle chili powder
½ tsp turmeric
½ tsp cumin
½ tsp chili flakes
½ tsp sea salt

1. In a large saucepan over medium-high heat, add half of the coconut oil and all of the kernels. Reduce heat to medium and let the kernels get hot, so they will start to pop. It will take about 7 minutes for them to start. Once they start popping, lift the pot and give it a little shake occasionally to ensure the kernels don't burn.

2. Meanwhile, in a small bowl, combine the nutritional yeast, paprika, chili powder, turmeric, cumin, chili flakes, and sea salt.

3. Once all kernels are popped, and the popping noise has slowed significantly, remove from the heat and transfer to a large bowl. Drizzle with the remaining coconut oil and add a generous sprinkling of your nutritional yeast mixture.

FOR THE CAULIFLOWER OPTION:

1. Substitute popcorn kernels for 1 head cauliflower cut into tiny bite-sized pieces. Preheat the oven to 425°F. Line a large baking sheet with parchment paper.

2. Evenly coat the cauliflower with the coconut oil and seasonings. Bake until golden (about 30 minutes).

SAUCES, SIDES, AND SNACKS | 183

184 | SAUCES, SIDES, AND SNACKS

Friday Night Dip

This is one of Erinn's favorite recipes. She's been making it since her university days and takes it to parties with friends and family. It's always been a hit! The layers look impressive and will be sure to dazzle the hardest-to-please guests. The kids will thank you for this when they come home from school. Three p.m. hunger pains solved!

PREP TIME: 15 minutes
BAKE TIME: 30 minutes
MAKES: 6 appetizer-size servings
SHELF LIFE: 2 days in the fridge

1 (14 oz) can refried black beans
6 avocados, peeled and pitted
2 Tbsp lime juice
¼ cup roughly chopped cilantro
1 cup vegan sour cream
1 tsp chipotle chili powder
1 tsp chili powder
3 tomatoes, roughly chopped
1 cup vegan cheese
1 bag of organic corn tortilla chips

1. Preheat the oven to 425°F.

2. Add the refried black beans to the bottom of a medium-size baking dish.

3. In a medium bowl, mash the avocados and lime juice with a fork until mixed together and still somewhat chunky. Stir in the cilantro.

4. Add the avocado mixture on top of the bean mixture and make sure it's spread evenly.

5. In a small bowl, combine the sour cream, chipotle powder, and chili pepper. Add the sour cream mixture over top the avocado mixture and spread evenly.

6. Add the tomatoes on top of the sour cream mixture, and again, spread evenly.

7. Finally, top with vegan cheese, and bake for 30 minutes uncovered, until edges start to bubble.

TO SERVE: Allow it to rest for 5 minutes before digging in. Serve with corn tortilla chips and enjoy! As an addition, you can enjoy with your favorite hot sauce or salsa.

NOTE: You can find plant-based sour cream and cheese readily available at every grocery store.

Quick and Easy Pickled Vegetables

While this recipe looks complex, it's actually so easy to make. Pickles are great for your gut health and can help aid in keeping your blood-sugar levels low. After having some digestive health issues, the past few years we've really learned to focus on taking good care of the gut (digestive tract). You can use these pickles with your favorite dips and spreads, in a salad, or on their own.

PREP TIME: 15 minutes
FERMENTING TIME: 1 day+
MAKES: 2 large mason jars
SHELF LIFE: 3 weeks in the fridge

4 cups filtered water

4 cups white vinegar or apple cider vinegar

4 Tbsp sea salt

½ cup organic sugar

1 Tbsp coriander seeds

1 tsp fennel seeds

1 tsp mustard seeds

7 cloves garlic, sliced lengthwise

½ red onion, sliced

Few sprigs fresh dill (optional)

About 6 cups of quartered fresh raw mixed veggies (we like beets, carrots, cucumbers, cauliflower, green beans, summer squash, and bell peppers)

Other optional additions: dill seeds, whole allspice, fresh ginger slices, chili flakes, peppercorns, cumin seeds, and other fresh herbs.

1. In a medium saucepan, bring the water, vinegar, salt, and sugar to a low boil until the salt and sugar dissolve. Once dissolved, let the liquid (brine or pickling liquid) cool for 10 minutes.

2. In two large sterilized mason jars, using sterilized tongs, begin to divide the coriander, fennel, mustard, garlic, red onion, dill, and other additions. You can then layer with the veggies and onions and repeat to have a pretty display. Or you could add the spices and herbs and then the veggies. Leave about 1 inch of room at the top.

3. Carefully pour the cooled pickling liquid into the jars, making sure the veggies are submerged. Once the liquid is added, you may be able to add more veggies to your jars.

4. Cover and let sit on the counter for a couple of hours. Then refrigerate for at least a day before consuming.

> **DYK:** Pickling was popular before the invention of refrigeration because canning and pickling helps to preserve vegetables. Pickled vegetables can last up to 5 to 6 months in your cold cellar pantry.

SAUCES, SIDES, AND SNACKS | 187

188 | SAUCES, SIDES, AND SNACKS

Oven-Roasted Tomatoes

This is such an easy recipe that gives so much back visually and also enhances the flavor of your meal. Kelly is a lover of fresh herbs. We pair these roasted tomatoes with our Creamy Polenta (page 158).

PREP TIME: 5 minutes
COOK TIME: 15–20 minutes
MAKES: ~2 cups
SHELF LIFE: 3 days in fridge

6 Roma tomatoes, cut lengthwise

2 Tbsp + 2 tsp extra-virgin olive oil, divided

4 cloves garlic, minced

1 Tbsp chopped fresh thyme

1 Tbsp chopped fresh rosemary

½ tsp dried basil

½ tsp sea salt, divided

1. Preheat the oven to 350°F. Line a baking sheet with parchment paper.

2. In a medium-size mixing bowl, add the tomatoes, 2 Tbsp of olive oil, garlic, thyme, rosemary, basil, and salt. Toss well. Arrange on the prepared baking sheet. Bake until tomatoes are soft and roasted, about 15 to 20 minutes.

3. Drizzle with remaining olive oil when the tomatoes come out of the oven. Serve on polenta or pasta or even as a side to a family meal.

SAUCES, SIDES, AND SNACKS

Classic Pesto

Kelly loves pesto! Even her pizzas are always green based. The freshness of the basil is what gets her every time. Stick with the freshest basil for the best-quality nutrients ... and pesto!

ACTIVE TIME: 7 minutes
TOTAL TIME: 10 minutes
MAKES: 1½ cups
SHELF LIFE: 1 week in the fridge

2 cups tightly packed fresh basil
½ cup pine nuts
2 cloves garlic, roughly chopped
1 Tbsp nutritional yeast
1 Tbsp lemon juice
½ tsp sea salt
½ cup extra-virgin olive oil

1. In a food processor, pulse the basil, pine nuts, garlic, nutritional yeast, lemon juice, and sea salt until smooth. With the processor running, slowly add the olive oil. Scrape down the sides of the food processor with a rubber spatula as needed.

TO SERVE: Use in your favorite recipe and enjoy.

DYK: You can swap out the pine nuts for ½ cup of sunflower seeds in this recipe for a nut-free option!

SAUCES, SIDES, AND SNACKS

Roasted Beet Hummus

A twist on traditional hummus, a vegan staple, this recipe is a beautiful addition to your daily routine and makes a pretty appetizer for your next dinner party.

PREP TIME: 15 minutes
BAKE TIME: 30–40 minutes
MAKES: about 2 cups of hummus
SHELF LIFE: 5 days in the fridge

1 medium beet, peeled and cut into chunks (about ¾ cup)

1 (19 oz) can chickpeas, drained and rinsed

2 cloves garlic

2 Tbsp tahini

Juice of 2 lemons

Sea salt and pepper, to taste

⅓ cup extra-virgin olive oil

1. Preheat the oven to 450°F. Line a baking dish with tin foil. Place your cut-up beet in the dish and cover with foil. Bake until the pieces are tender (about 30–40 minutes). Remove from oven, and let sit for 5 minutes.

2. While the beets are cooling, blend the chickpeas, garlic, and tahini in a food processor until smooth (about 2 minutes). Add the lemon juice, salt, and pepper. Blend again for 10 seconds. Slowly add the olive oil and blend until smooth.

3. Once the beets have cooled, add to the food processor. Blend until smooth.

TO SERVE: Chill in the fridge, then serve with a drizzle of EVOO, sesame seeds and your favorite crackers or Kale Chips (page 177). Can be stored for up to 5 days in the fridge.

Easy Cheese Sauce

This cheese sauce is the best we've ever had. And it's made with carrots and potatoes! Yep! We love how simple it is to make and how delicious it is. Use it with our Sweet Potato Nachos (page 165).

PREP TIME: 15 minutes
COOK TIME: 15 minutes
MAKES: 3 cups
SHELF LIFE: 3 days in the fridge

2 Tbsp peeled and chopped shallots
1 cup peeled and chopped russet potatoes
1 cup filtered water
⅓ cup onion, peeled and chopped
2 large carrots, peeled and chopped
¼ cup raw cashews
1 tsp sea salt
¼ tsp minced garlic
⅓ cup vegan butter
¼ tsp Dijon mustard
1 Tbsp lemon juice
¼ tsp black pepper
⅛ tsp cayenne
⅛ tsp smoked paprika
⅛ tsp turmeric
2 Tbsp nutritional yeast
2 Tbsp coconut oil

1. In a saucepan over medium heat, add the shallots, potatoes, water, onion, and carrots, and bring to a boil. Cover and simmer until the vegetables are very soft (about 15 minutes).

2. Meanwhile, in a heavy-duty blender on high speed, blend the cashews, sea salt, garlic, butter, mustard, lemon juice, black pepper, cayenne, paprika, turmeric, nutritional yeast, and coconut oil. Add softened vegetables and cooking water to the blender in batches, and process until perfectly smooth.

TO SERVE: Use in your favorite recipe. Some people like to eat it by the spoonful. We won't name any names.

SAUCES, SIDES, AND SNACKS | 195

Turmeric Miso Sauce

We love this sauce, and it's so versatile and great on a wide variety of plant-based bowls.

PREP TIME: 5 minutes
MAKES: 1½ cups
SHELF LIFE: 1 week in the fridge

1 Tbsp yellow miso

½ cup tahini

¾ cup warm filtered water

1 tsp finely grated fresh ginger

½ tsp turmeric powder or ½ tsp finely grated fresh turmeric

1 tsp lemon juice

1 clove minced garlic

Pinch of black pepper

Sea salt, to taste

1. In a heavy-duty blender, blend all of the ingredients until smooth.

2. Add a little water if the sauce is too thick for your liking.

TO SERVE: Enjoy it with EVERYTHING!

NOTE: For a soy-free version, sub the yellow miso with chickpea miso, available at your local health-food store.

Almond Ginger Dressing

This is a rich and flavorful dressing that will liven up your salad greens.

PREP TIME: 5 minutes
MAKES: ½ cup
SHELF LIFE: 1 week in the fridge

3 Tbsp almond butter

1 Tbsp minced ginger

1 lime, zested and juiced

2 Tbsp extra-virgin olive oil

2 Tbsp filtered water

2 tsp sesame oil

1 Tbsp wheat-free tamari

2 tsp chili flakes

1. In a heavy-duty blender on high speed, blend all of the ingredients until smooth (about 30 seconds).

The Best Vegan Mayo

This is a tried-and-true recipe from the Kindfood and Lettuce Love Cafe days, which everyone loved! It is used on our B.L.A.T. sandwiches (page 166).

PREP TIME: 10 minutes
MAKES: 1 cup
SHELF LIFE: 1 week in the fridge

- ½ cup unsweetened original soy milk
- 1 tsp Dijon mustard
- 1 Tbsp lemon juice
- ¾ tsp sea salt
- ¼ tsp apple cider vinegar
- ¾ cup grapeseed oil, avocado oil, or non-GMO canola oil

1. Chill the soy milk in the fridge for 30 minutes before using, to make it extra cold.

2. In a medium bowl, mix the mustard, lemon juice, sea salt, and apple cider vinegar. Add the chilled soy milk and whisk well.

3. Pour the milk mixture into a food processor and *slowly* add the oil until emulsified. Check consistency frequently. When emulsified completely, a spoon should be able to create a trench that doesn't collapse in the mayo.

Lemon Tahini Dressing

This versatile dressing works on pretty much every kind of salad. It is such a flavorful dressing.

PREP TIME: 5 minutes
MAKES: 2 cups
SHELF LIFE: 1 week in the fridge

- 1 cup tahini
- ⅓ cup lemon juice
- 1 tsp garlic
- 1 tsp sea salt
- 1 tsp tamari
- ½ tsp cayenne
- ¾ cup filtered water

1. In a heavy-duty blender or mixing bowl, blend or whisk all of the ingredients until a creamy dressing is formed.

Our Famous Brazil Nut Parmesan

This makes a savory, tasty addition to everything from salads to pasta to sandwiches. We make it and keep a supply in the freezer to pull and use as necessary. It stays fresh that way. There are so many ways to enjoy it. Trust us, this parmesan is a must for ALL Caesar Salads. Brazil nuts are high in selenium, which is great for the prostate. Also, these nuts are calorie-dense with a lot of monounsaturated fats—the fats that encourage good cholesterol instead of clogging your arteries. This recipe is also in our first cookbook, *Made with Love*, but we wanted to add it again, since you all loved it so much.

ACTIVE TIME: 5–8 minutes
MAKES: 2 cups
SHELF LIFE: 7–10 days in the fridge or freezer for 2 months

2 cups Brazil nuts
½ cup nutritional yeast
1 large garlic clove, minced
¾ tsp sea salt

> DYK: Brazil nuts are the highest natural source of selenium, a mineral that has been known to help prevent coronary artery disease and prostate cancer. Just one or two nuts a day provides enough selenium to make a difference to your health.

1. Pulse the Brazil nuts in a very dry food processor fitted with the metallic blade. Make sure there is no moisture in the processor, or you will end up with Brazil nut butter.

2. Keep pulsing until nuts are evenly crumbled.

3. Add the nutritional yeast, minced garlic, and salt. Pulse two or three times to toss the garlic and salt through the nuts.

4. Pour the nut parmesan into two glass storage containers with tight lids: One container is for the fridge and the other is to store the parmesan in the freezer to use as needed. It will keep in the refrigerator for 7–10 days and the freezer for 2 months.

This is our national best-selling first cookbook, *Made with Love*, published in 2016.

SAUCES, SIDES, AND SNACKS | 199

BROWN RICE SYRUP
This is a natural sweetener that's fairly low on the glycemic index.

GLUTEN-FREE FLOURS
we use Bob's Red Mill flours, mainly their garbanzo fava bean flours and their all-purpose flour blend!

Plant-based Baking Essentials

These are a few of our favorite items to keep stocked in our pantry at home, for more information visit our pantry at the beginning of the book.

SUCANAT
Naturally processed cane sugar. Sucanat is the rawest form of cane sugar and still has plenty of micronutrients intact.

Our favorite Canadian staple sweetener. We love using maple syrup instead of cane sugar where we can.

MAPLE SYRUP

SWEET POTATO PUREE — another great moisture-adding ingredient that's high in fiber and beta-carotene.

We use fair trade and organic sugars in all of our baking at Kelly's Bake Shoppe. For us, it's always been important to make sure people are paid fair wages to produce our ingredients in other countries.

ORGANIC CANE SUGAR

CHIA SEEDS — one of our favorite egg replacers. 1 Tbsp of chia seeds with 3 Tbsp of water = 1 egg!

VEGAN CHOCOLATE CHIPS — our favorite brand for vegan chocolate chips is Enjoy Life. We've been using them since 2010.

APPLE SAUCE — great egg replacers when you're in a pinch. Also, it adds great moisture to your baking.

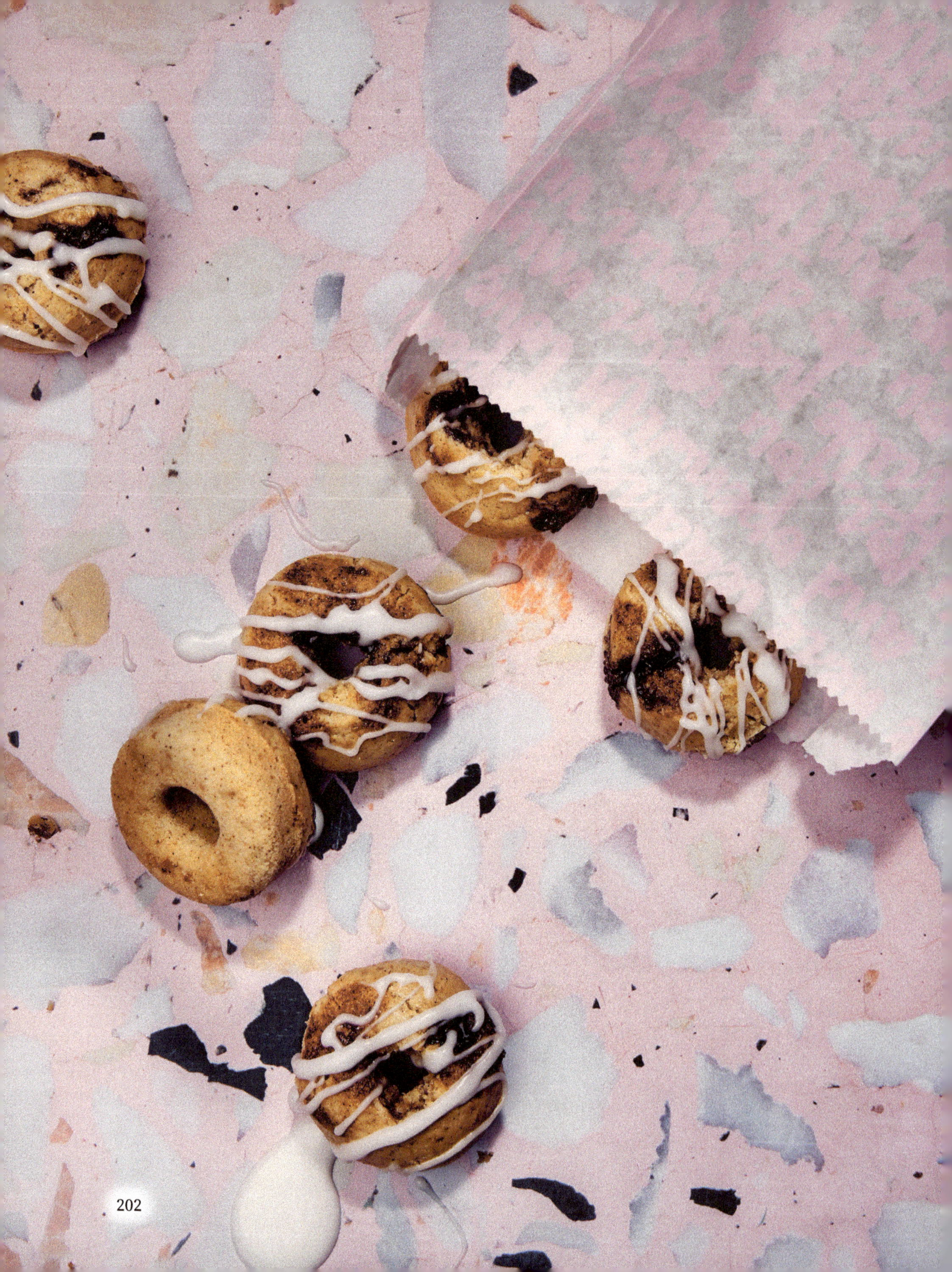

Desserts

Sugar Cookies with Pumpkin Frosting 205

Manuka Honey Baked Figs 209

The Skinny Cookie 2.0 211

Ginger Molasses Cookies 212

Compost Cookies 213

Indulgent Shortbread Cookies 214

Matcha Shortbread 217

Chocolate Chunk Turmeric Cookies 219

Best Banana Bread 220

"Can't Handle this Jelly" Muffins 223

S'mores Cupcakes 227

Chocolate-Dipped Macaroons 228

Cinnamon Bun Donuts 229

Magical Chocolate Birthday Cake 233

Strawberry Shortcake 236

Summer Peach Crumble 239

Matcha Nice Cream 241

Whipped Cream 242

Simple Vanilla Buttercream 243

Raw Date Sauce 244

Sugar-Free Frosting 245

Cacao Sauce 246

DESSERTS

Sugar Cookies with Pumpkin Frosting

Melt-in-your-mouth sugar cookies topped with pumpkin frosting is all you really need in life, right? This recipe is our go-to for a versatile sugar cookie that goes well with just about anything.

PREP TIME: 10 minutes
CHILL TIME: 3 hours
BAKE TIME: 15 minutes
MAKES: about 1 dozen cookies
SHELF LIFE: 3 days in the cookie jar or 1 week in the freezer

COOKIES:

½ cup + 1 Tbsp organic sugar

⅓ cup Sucanat

½ cup coconut oil, softened

⅓ cup applesauce, room temperature

2 tsp pure vanilla extract

1¾ cup gluten-free all-purpose flour

½ Tbsp arrowroot starch

1½ tsp baking powder

¼ tsp sea salt

FOR THE COOKIES:

1. In a medium bowl, using an electric hand mixer, cream the sugar, Sucanat, and coconut oil. Mix in the applesauce and vanilla.

2. Using an electric hand mixer or spatula, mix in the flour, arrowroot starch, baking powder, and sea salt, ensuring that there is no residual oil on the top of the bowl.

3. Refrigerate the dough for a minimum of 3 hours.

4. When ready to bake, preheat the oven to 350°F. Line a baking sheet with parchment paper.

5. Using 2 tablespoons, form the dough into balls, and place about 2 inches apart on the prepared baking sheet. Press down the cookies to 1-inch thickness and bake until slightly golden (about 10 to 12 minutes). Allow cookies to cool.

recipe continued

FROSTING:

½ cup vegan butter, softened

1 Tbsp pumpkin puree

2½ cups powdered sugar

A splash of Coconut Milk (page 52) (optional)

¼ tsp ground cinnamon

¼ tsp pumpkin pie spice

½ tsp vanilla extract

FOR THE FROSTING:

1. In a medium bowl, using an electric hand mixer, beat the softened butter and pumpkin puree until light and fluffy. Add the powdered sugar slowly and continue mixing until thick and creamy. Drizzle a little coconut milk if the frosting is too thick. Alternatively, add more powdered sugar if the frosting gets too thin. Add the cinnamon, pumpkin pie spice, and vanilla, and mix until combined.

TO SERVE: Frost the cookies with a healthy serving of pumpkin frosting using a butterknife.

DESSERTS | 207

DESSERTS

Manuka Honey Baked Figs

Simple and decadent. We make this for Sunday brunch or a quick and easy after work or school snack. Figs are great for heart health, loaded with antioxidants and rich in fiber, which helps to promote good digestion. Eating a diet that's rich in figs can help "keep you regular."

PREP TIME: 3 minutes
BAKE TIME: 10 minutes
MAKES: 4 servings
SHELF LIFE: 2 days in the fridge

8 fresh figs, halved
½ cup orange juice
2 Tbsp Manuka honey
1 Tbsp finely sliced orange rind
2 sticks cinnamon

1. Preheat the oven to 350°F. Grease a casserole dish (that has a cover) with coconut oil non-stick spray.

2. Place all of the ingredients into the prepared casserole dish and stir to coat the figs in the honey mixture.

3. Bake for 5 minutes covered, and then uncover and continue another 5 minutes until the figs are slightly golden.

TO SERVE: Transfer to a plate and serve with the remaining drizzle from the dish. This dessert works well with a side of vanilla ice cream.

210 | DESSERTS

The Skinny Cookie 2.0

This is a version of our most popular cookie at Kelly's Bake Shoppe since its release in 2012. The original Skinny Cookie is top secret and as many of you know, flourless and cane sugar-free! In this cookbook version we've added some additional nutrient dense ingredients, that's why we call it the Skinny Cookie 2.0!

PREP TIME: 10 minutes
BAKE TIME: 15 minutes
ROASTING TIME: 20 minutes
MAKES: 1 dozen cookies
SHELF LIFE: 1 month in the freezer

3 bananas
¼ cup coconut sugar
1 cup + 2 Tbsp gluten-free rolled oats
½ cup shredded coconut
3 Tbsp hemp seeds
½ tsp baking powder
⅛ tsp cinnamon
½ tsp sea salt
¾ cup sunflower seed butter/almond butter/cashew butter/peanut butter
¼ cup coconut oil, softened
1 tsp vanilla extract
⅓ cup chocolate chips
⅓ cup dried cranberries
¼ cup chopped almonds

1. Preheat the oven to 400°F. Line a baking sheet with parchment paper.

2. Place the bananas (peels on) on the prepared sheet and roast for 20 minutes. Transfer to a plate and allow to cool.

3. Lower the oven temperature to 350°F. Line a baking sheet with parchment paper.

4. In a medium bowl, combine the coconut sugar, rolled oats, shredded coconut, hemp seeds, baking powder, cinnamon, and sea salt.

5. Once the bananas have cooled, peel and add to a large bowl. Using a hand mixer, combine with the sunflower seed butter, coconut oil, and vanilla.

6. Add the dry ingredients to the wet ingredients and mix well with a rubber spatula. Fold in the chocolate chips, cranberries, and almonds.

7. Using an ice-cream scoop, spoon the dough on the prepared baking sheet, placing about 1 inch apart. Press the scooped dough down to ½ inch thickness and bake until the edges are golden brown (about 10 to 12 minutes). Store in a covered container in the refrigerator for up to 5 days or in the freezer for a month.

Ginger Molasses Cookies

This is one of the fan-favorite seasonal cookies at Kelly's Bake Shoppe. Made with freshly grated ginger and powdered ginger and topped with candied ginger, they're the perfect fall treat. We have had so many requests for this recipe that we can't keep it secret any longer!

PREP TIME: 10 minutes
BAKE TIME: 10–12 minutes
CHILL TIME: 20 minutes
MAKES: about 1 dozen cookies
SHELF LIFE: 3 days in the cookie jar or 1 week in the freezer

2 Tbsp flax meal

⅓ cup filtered water

½ cup softened vegan butter

¾ cup coconut sugar

¼ cup molasses

1 Tbsp fresh grated ginger

1 tsp vanilla

2 cups gluten-free all-purpose flour

1 tsp ginger

1 tsp cinnamon

1 ½ tsp baking soda

¼ tsp sea salt

Organic cane sugar, for rolling

Candied ginger, for topping

1. In a small bowl, combine the flax meal and water. Set aside for 2 to 3 minutes.

2. In a medium bowl, cream the vegan butter and coconut sugar. Then add the flax mixture, molasses, fresh ginger, and vanilla. Using a hand mixer, beat until blended.

3. In another bowl, combine the flour, powdered ginger, cinnamon, baking soda, and sea salt.

4. Add the dry ingredients to the wet ingredients and mix well by hand or using a rubber spatula.

5. Let the dough rest, covered, for 20 minutes in the fridge.

6. Meanwhile, preheat the oven to 350°F. Line a baking sheet with parchment paper.

7. Using a tablespoon, form the dough into a dozen balls. Roll each ball in the organic cane sugar and press the cookies down to a 1-inch thickness. Place them on the prepared baking sheet about 2 inches apart. Press a candied ginger into each cookie.

8. Bake for 10 to 12 minutes. Let cool before serving.

TO SERVE: Indulge in the cooled cookies right away and maybe dip them in your favorite non-dairy milk? YUM! You can also freeze for a later date.

Compost Cookies

We came across this cookie through our travels on Vancouver Island. It was one of the favorite things we ate while we were away—so much so that we came home and made our own version to share with you! You can go crazy with this cookie. You know why? You can add anything!! Pretzels, peanuts, potato chips, sunflower seeds, cereals, chopped dates, coconut, chopped dark chocolate.... That's why they call it the "Compost" Cookie!

PREP TIME: 10 minutes
BAKE TIME: 10–12 minutes
MAKES: about 2 dozen cookies
SHELF LIFE: 3 days in the cookie jar or 1 month in the freezer

1 tsp chia seeds

2 Tbsp filtered water

½ cup + 1 Tbsp smooth almond butter

½ cup pure maple syrup

3 Tbsp Sucanat

3 Tbsp coconut oil, softened

½ tsp pure vanilla extract

½ cup gluten-free rolled oats

½ cup gluten-free all-purpose flour

½ tsp baking soda

¼ cup arrowroot starch

½ tsp sea salt

¼ cup vegan dark chocolate chips

¼ cup flaked coconut

¼ cup pumpkin seeds

¼ cup gluten-free pretzels, crushed

½ cup add-ins of your choice (vegan chocolate, dates, nuts, seeds, etc.)

1. Preheat the oven to 375°F. Line two baking sheets with parchment paper.

2. In a small bowl, combine the chia seeds and filtered water. Set aside.

3. In a large mixing bowl, and using an electric hand mixer, mix together the almond butter, maple syrup, Sucanat, coconut oil, and vanilla. Add the chia mixture to the almond butter mixture.

4. In a medium mixing bowl, whisk together the oats, flour, baking soda, arrowroot, and sea salt.

5. Add the dry ingredients to wet ingredients. Mix well using a wooden spoon or spatula. Stir chia seed mixture into the batter.

6. Stir in the chocolate chips, flaked coconut, pumpkin seeds, pretzels, and about ½ cup of any additions you'd like for your cookies. Mix well.

7. Using a tablespoon, scoop out the cookie dough onto the prepared baking sheets, 12 per tray and about 1-inch apart.

8. Bake until golden brown (about 8 to 10 minutes).

TO SERVE: Let cool for 5 to 6 minutes and enjoy! Enjoy them warm from the oven.

Indulgent Shortbread Cookies

Our classic shortbread cookie. For this recipe, we've enhanced it with a little cracked sea salt and chocolate chunks. Why? Because the taste of cracked salt compliments a cookie so well and makes us pucker up. It's delicious!

PREP TIME: 10 minutes
BAKE TIME: 10–12 minutes
CHILL TIME: 3 hours
MAKES: 12 cookies
SHELF LIFE: 1 month in the freezer

½ cup + 1 Tbsp organic sugar

⅓ cup organic Sucanat (see note on page 221)

½ cup coconut oil

⅓ cup applesauce, at room temperature

2 tsp vanilla

1¾ cups gluten-free all-purpose flour

½ Tbsp arrowroot starch

1½ tsp baking powder

¼ tsp sea salt

½ cup vegan chocolate chips (We love Enjoy Life brand.)

1 tsp flaked sea salt

VARIATION: LEMONY SHORTBREAD COOKIES

Add 1 Tbsp lemon zest with 2 tsp lemon extract. Omit the chocolate chips and flaked sea salt.

1. In a medium bowl, using an electric hand mixer, cream the organic sugar, Sucanat, and coconut oil. Add the applesauce and vanilla and continue to mix thoroughly.

2. In another medium bowl, combine the flour, arrowroot starch, baking powder, and salt.

3. Add the dry ingredients to the wet ingredients and mix well with a hand mixer, ensuring there is no residual oil on the top of the bowl.

4. Fold in the chocolate chips and mix until incorporated.

5. Form the dough into a large ball, wrap in plastic wrap, and refrigerate for a minimum of 3 hours and maximum of 24 hours.

6. When ready to bake, preheat the oven to 350°F. Line a baking sheet with parchment paper. Place another piece of parchment paper on a work surface and roll out the cookie dough to 1-inch thickness. Cut with a cookie cutter of choice. Top each cookie with a pinch of flaked sea salt. Bake until golden (about 10 to 12 minutes).

NOTE: If you want to get a dose of antioxidants, check out our next recipe, Matcha Shortbread! (page 217)

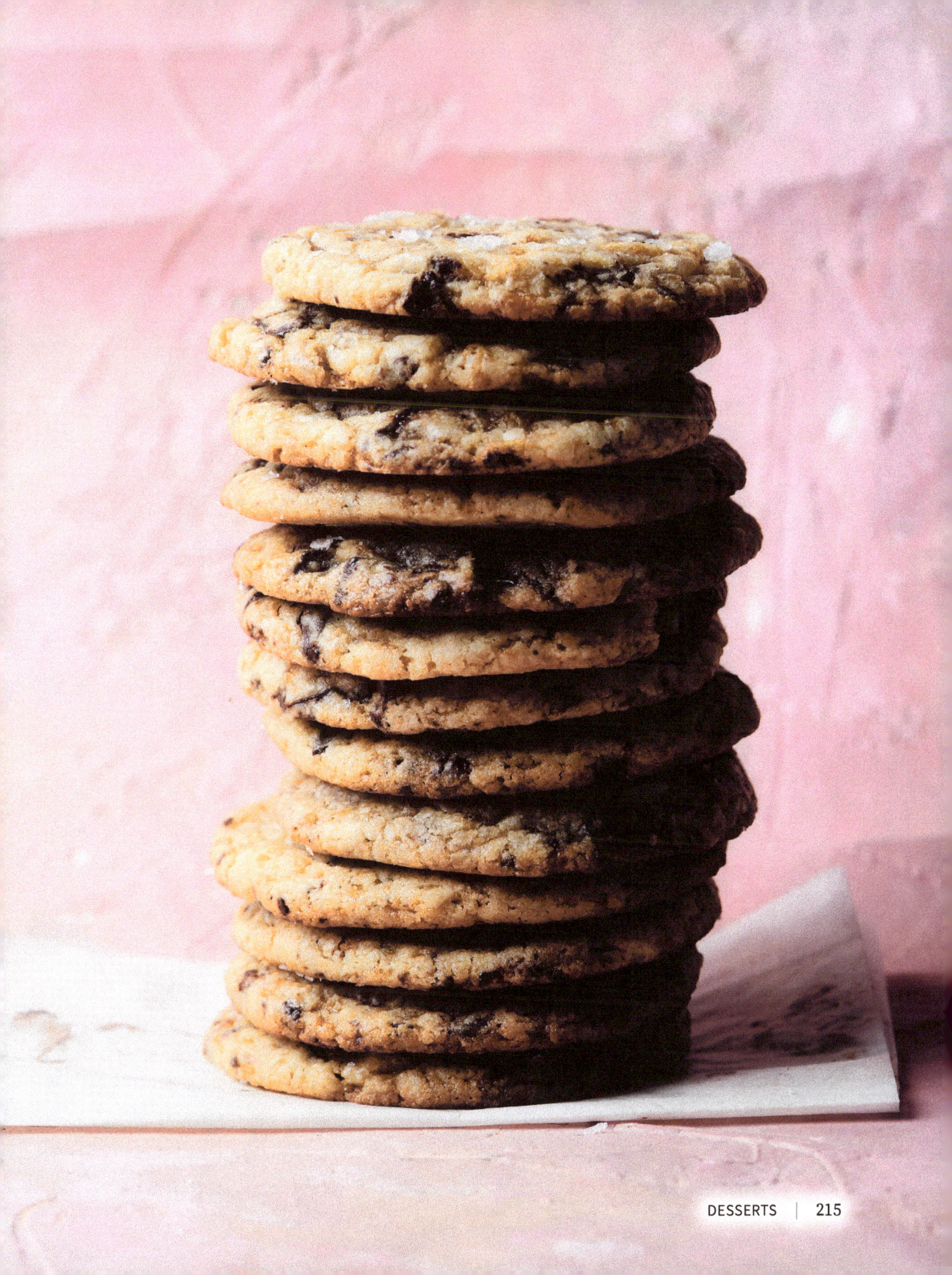

216 | DESSERTS

Matcha Shortbread

Our Matcha Shortbread is an all-time fan-favorite cookie at Kelly's Bake Shoppe. This recipe is an easier but just as delicious version as the one at the shoppe. When we first released this cookie around Christmas of 2018, we couldn't keep up with the demand. We sold literally hundreds upon hundreds a day. Wowweeeee! We even ran out of large Matcha powder bags every three days! We couldn't believe it, and … just saying … it definitely started a craze!

PREP TIME: 20 minutes
BAKE TIME: 12 minutes
MAKES: 12–15 cookies
SHELF LIFE: 3 days in the cookie jar or 2 months in the freezer

1 cup coconut oil, softened
½ cup organic cane sugar
¼ cup powdered sugar
1 tsp pure vanilla extract
2 cups gluten-free all-purpose flour
1 Tbsp ceremonial grade matcha powder
¼ tsp sea salt

OPTIONAL DIPPING:

1 cup chocolate chips
1 tsp coconut oil
1 Tbsp flaked sea salt

1. Preheat the oven to 350° F. Line a baking sheet with parchment paper.

2. In a medium bowl, using a hand mixer, cream the softened coconut oil, sugar, powdered sugar and vanilla.

3. In another medium bowl, whisk together the gluten-free flour, matcha powder, and salt.

4. Add the dry ingredients to the wet ingredients and mix with a hand mixer. It will be coarse and crumbly but can still be shaped. Use your hands to form the dough into a ball.

5. Place a piece of parchment on a rolling surface and roll out the dough on top of it, using a floured rolling pin. Roll to ½-inch thickness.

6. Cut with a cookie cutter—we use a 3-inch cutter at Kelly's Bake Shoppe (dip in flour after every press)—or use a knife to draw lines and create bars.

7. Bake for 12 to 13 minutes and let cool.

TO SERVE: Dig in now, or if desired, in a small saucepan over very low heat, melt the chocolate chips and coconut oil, stirring with a spatula. Dip the cooled cookies or bars into the chocolate, set on parchment paper, and sprinkle with flaked sea salt. Let cool at room temperature.

DESSERTS

Chocolate Chunk Turmeric Cookies

The best of both worlds: the indulgence of chocolate with the anti-inflammatory properties of turmeric. These cookies are also packed with tons of fiber and protein thanks to the oat and almond flour.

PREP TIME: 10 minutes
BAKE TIME: 14 minutes
MAKES: 1 dozen cookies
SHELF LIFE: 3 days in the cookie jar or 1 month in the freezer

½ cup natural, smooth cashew butter or sunflower seed butter

½ cup maple syrup

3½ Tbsp virgin coconut oil, softened

1 tsp vanilla

½ cup gluten-free rolled oats

¼ cup + 3 Tbsp gluten-free oat flour

¼ cup arrowroot starch or tapioca starch

¼ cup almond flour or coconut flour

½ tsp baking soda

½ tsp sea salt

2 tsp turmeric

¾ cup chocolate chunks + 3 Tbsp, for garnish (We love Enjoy Life or Cocoa Camino brand.)

1. Preheat the oven to 350°F. Line a large baking sheet with parchment paper.

2. In a large bowl, stir together the cashew butter or sunflower seed butter, maple syrup, coconut oil, and vanilla until completely smooth.

3. In a medium bowl, whisk together the oats, oat flour, arrowroot or tapioca starch, almond or coconut flour, baking soda, sea salt, and turmeric.

4. Add the dry mixture to the wet mixture using a spatula to fold in until thoroughly combined. It is normal for the dough to be a bit oily or wet.

5. Stir the chocolate chunks into the dough until combined.

6. Using a tablespoon, scoop about 2 tablespoons of dough per cookie, about 2 inches apart, onto the prepared baking sheet.

7. Press 3 chocolate chunks into each cookie. (This is how we do it at Kelly's Bake Shoppe.)

8. Bake until the cookies spread out (about 10 to 12 minutes). For a crispier cookie, bake for about 12–14 minutes.

TO SERVE: Allow cookies to cool and indulge immediately or freeze for a later date.

Best Banana Bread

There's nothing like freshly baked banana bread, warm from the oven. To make sure it's moist and delicious, be sure to use browned, ripened (overripe is fine) bananas. The roasting of the banana ahead of time brings out their sweet richness.

PREP TIME: 15 minutes
BAKE TIME: 20 minutes
ROASTING TIME: 20 minutes
MAKES: about 2 dozen muffins or 2 large loaves
SHELF LIFE: 1 week in the freezer

2 cups bananas (about 6 bananas)
¾ cup Coconut Milk (page 52)
½ tsp apple cider vinegar
3 cups gluten-free all-purpose flour
2½ tsp baking powder
2½ tsp baking soda
½ tsp sea salt
½ tsp cinnamon
¾ cup sunflower or coconut oil, melted
¾ cup Sucanat or coconut sugar
⅓ cup + 1 Tbsp apple sauce
1 tsp vanilla
1 cup walnuts or pecans, crushed (optional)
1 cup chocolate chips (optional)

1. Preheat the oven to 350°F. Roast the bananas for 20 minutes in a 9 x 13-inch roasting pan. Let cool, peel, and toss out banana skins. Set the roasted bananas aside in a small bowl.

2. Lightly spray two 12-cup muffin pans or two large loaf pans with cooking spray, or line them with paper liners.

3. In a small bowl, add the coconut milk and apple cider vinegar, let sit for 5 minutes.

4. In a medium bowl, whisk together the flour, baking powder, baking soda, sea salt, and cinnamon.

5. In a large bowl, and using an electric hand mixer on medium speed, beat the oil, Sucanat, apple sauce, and vanilla. Stir in the coconut milk and vinegar mixture and the roasted bananas.

6. Add the flour mixture to the wet ingredients and mix well with a hand mixer.

7. Gently fold in the nuts and chocolate chips, if using.

8. Using an ice-cream scoop (our favorite kitchen tool at the Bake Shoppe), spoon the batter into the prepared muffin pan or pour into a loaf pan.

9. Bake until a knife or toothpick comes out clean (about 20 to 22 minutes).

10. Let cool for 5 to 10 minutes before eating.

NOTE: Sucanat is the raw form of cane sugar. It's a version of cane sugar that still contains the natural molasses and traces of nutrients like iron, calcium, and potassium. It's also preferred by many people following a plant-based lifestyle as the processing of it doesn't require animal bone char. It is available for purchase at natural-food stores and grocery stores.

222 | DESSERTS

"Can't Handle this Jelly" Muffins

Kelly made jelly-filled muffins in her grade-seven Home Economics class, a memory that always stayed with her. It's funny how, when we reflect on our lives, it's not what we did but how we felt doing it that sticks with us. This class, for Kelly, was magical. It was a chance to perfect her baking skills and do a little dreaming; it made her FEEL so connected to her happy button. Inspired by these memories and named after that Destiny's Child lyric (because why not?), we think these will not only nourish but inspire new memories.

PREP TIME: 15–20 minutes
BAKE TIME: 15 minutes
MAKES: 12–14 muffins
SHELF LIFE: 1 month in the freezer

1 Tbsp flaxseed meal

1 Tbsp chia seeds

4 Tbsp filtered water

½ cup Coconut Milk (page 52) or canned

1 tsp apple cider vinegar

¼ cup apple sauce

¼ cup coconut oil, melted

¼ cup brown rice syrup

½ cup organic cane sugar

1 cup gluten-free all-purpose flour

⅔ cup almond meal

½ cup rolled oats

½ cup shredded unsweetened coconut

2½ tsp baking powder

1½ tsp baking soda

½ tsp sea salt

¼ tsp xanthan gum

6 tsp fruit jam (We love blueberry, cherry, strawberry, or raspberry!)

GARNISH

3 strawberries, quartered

12 raspberries

1. Preheat the oven to 375°F. Lightly spray a 12-cup muffin pan with cooking spray or line it with paper liners.

2. In a large mixing bowl, combine the flaxseed meal, chia seeds and filtered water. Let sit for 5 minutes.

3. In a small mixing bowl, add the coconut milk and apple cider vinegar. Let sit for 5 minutes.

4. Add the coconut milk mixture to the flaxseed mixture. Add the applesauce, coconut oil, brown rice syrup, and cane sugar. Blend with an electric hand mixer for 30 seconds.

5. In a medium bowl, whisk together the all-purpose flour, almond meal, oats, shredded coconut, baking powder, baking soda, sea salt, and xanthan gum.

recipe continued

6. Add the dry ingredients to the wet ingredients. Beat with an electric hand mixer until thoroughly combined.

7. Using an ice-cream scoop, spoon the batter into the prepared muffin pan.

8. Add ½ tsp of jam to the top of each muffin. It will sink a little when baking. Top each muffin with a strawberry and raspberry.

9. Bake until a toothpick inserted into the center comes out clean and the edges are golden brown (about 15 minutes). Let cool for 15 minutes before gently removing from the pan, then let cool completely on a cooling rack.

TO SERVE: Eat them right away or freeze for snacks! We love having a stash of these in our freezer.

NOTE: If you're feeling adventurous, place a small dollop of some sunflower seed butter or almond butter on these muffins for a PB&J taste!

DESSERTS | 225

226 | DESSERTS

S'mores Cupcakes

The S'mores cupcake is reminiscent of cottage life, bonfires, and starry summer nights at the cottage. Ohhhhh, take us back there!

PREP TIME: 25 minutes
BAKE TIME: 20–25 minutes
MAKES: 24 cupcakes
SHELF LIFE: 2 months in the freezer

2½ cups gluten-free all-purpose flour

2 tsp baking powder

½ tsp baking soda

½ tsp sea salt

¼ tsp xanthan gum

2 cups Coconut Milk (page 52) or store-bought coconut beverage

2 tsp apple cider vinegar

1 cup organic cane sugar

½ cup Sucanat

¾ cup non-GMO canola oil or another neutral oil of your choice

2 tsp vanilla extract

½ bag vegan mini marshmallows (Dandies are our favorite.)

½ cup Cacao Sauce (page 246)

4 cups Vanilla Buttercream (page 243)

24 store-bought graham crackers

1. Preheat the oven to 350°F. Spray 2 muffin pans with cooking spray or line with cupcake liners.

2. In a large bowl, whisk together the flour, baking powder, baking soda, sea salt, and xanthan gum.

3. In a small bowl, combine the coconut milk and apple cider vinegar. Let sit for a couple of minutes.

4. In another large bowl, using an electric hand mixer, blend the cane sugar, Sucanat, canola oil, and vanilla extract. Add the coconut milk and apple cider vinegar and beat with the hand mixer.

5. Add the dry ingredients to the wet ingredients and beat on high for 2 to 3 minutes, until all the lumps are gone, and the batter is smooth.

6. Using an ice-cream scoop, divide the batter among the cupcake liners.

7. Bake until a sharp knife comes out clean (about 20 to 25 minutes). Do not overbake. Allow the cupcakes to cool slightly.

8. While the cupcakes are still warm, poke a hole with a clean finger, and fill each with 3 marshmallows. Let cupcakes cool for an hour.

TO SERVE: Once the cupcakes are cooled, frost with vanilla buttercream. Drizzle with Cacao Sauce (page 246) using a spoon, and then top each cupcake with a graham cracker. Voila! Instant Cottage Living!

Chocolate-Dipped Macaroons

This is one of our original Kindfood cafe recipes. Our intention was to sell these macaroons to customers, but we would secretly eat about ten of them a day since we wouldn't have a second to sit down and eat a proper meal. We vividly remember those days of waking up at 3:00 a.m. to bake cupcakes, cookies, and brownies, and then at 9:00 a.m., having to switch gears to set up the kitchen for lunch service. Oh, the life of a business owner.

PREP TIME: 7 minutes
BAKE TIME: 12 minutes
CHILL TIME: 1 hour
MAKES: About 1 dozen
SHELF LIFE: 4 days at room temperature or 1 month in the freezer

1 Tbsp white chia seeds
1¼ cup short, unsweetened, shredded coconut
⅓ cup maple syrup or brown rice syrup
¼ cup + 2 Tbsp coconut oil, softened and divided
¼ cup coconut flour or almond flour
1 cup chocolate chips
¼ tsp sea salt

1. Preheat the oven to 325°F. Line a baking sheet with parchment paper.

2. In a medium bowl, combine the chia seeds, coconut, maple syrup, ¼ cup of coconut oil, and flour, and mix well with your hands.

3. Wet your hands with water and form the mixture into heaping tablespoon-sized balls.

4. Bake until the macaroons are golden brown (about 10 to 12 minutes).

5. Meanwhile, in a double boiler, over medium heat, melt the remaining 2 Tbsp of coconut oil and then add the chocolate chips, and sea salt. Let them melt, stirring occasionally. Remove from heat once melted.

6. Let the baked macaroons cool. Meanwhile, line the baking sheet with wax paper.

7. Dip the macaroon bottoms into the melted chocolate. Place onto the prepared baking sheet and let set for 10 to 15 minutes.

TO SERVE: Chill in the fridge for 1 hour to harden the chocolate. Enjoy!

Cinnamon Bun Donuts

We were trying to nail down an epic plant-based and gluten-free cinnamon bun for years but had always found that they would turn out really hard and dense. Finally though, through endless perseverance, we've made these epic cinnamon bun donuts that we think are better than the bun version! These are more divine than we could have ever imagined. It is definitely in the Cinnamon Topping and glaze! We think you'll love them!

PREP TIME: 20 minutes
BAKE TIME: 20 minutes
MAKES: 12–16 mini-donuts
SHELF LIFE: 1 week in the freezer

CINNAMON TOPPING

2 Tbsp vegan butter

2 tsp cinnamon

5 Tbsp Sucanat (see note on page 221)

1 tsp Coconut Milk (page 52) or store bought

1 tsp arrowroot starch

1 tsp vanilla

DONUTS

1¼ cups gluten-free all-purpose flour

1 tsp baking powder

¼ tsp baking soda

½ tsp sea salt

½ tsp cinnamon

½ cup cane sugar

¼ cup Sucanat

⅓ cup melted coconut oil or non-GMO canola oil

1 cup Coconut Milk (page 52)

1 tsp vanilla

FOR THE CINNAMON TOPPING:

1. In a small saucepan over low heat, melt the butter. Stir in the cinnamon, Sucanat, coconut milk, and arrowroot starch.

2. Heat until it begins to boil. Remove from heat and stir in the vanilla. Set aside.

FOR THE DONUTS:

1. Preheat the oven to 350°F. Grease a mini-donut pan or mini-cupcake pan with non-stick spray.

2. In a medium sized bowl, mix together the flour, baking powder, baking soda, sea salt, cinnamon, cane sugar, Sucanat.

3. In another bowl, mix together the oil, milk and vanilla.

recipe continued

DESSERTS | 229

4. Add dry ingredients to the wet ingredients and mix well with a hand mixer until thoroughly combined.

5. Using a small ice cream scoop, portion a small amount of batter into each mini-donut well. Don't overfill. Top with a little cinnamon topping.

6. Bake until slightly browned, about 8 minutes.

7. Remove from the oven and let cool.

GLAZE

1 cup powdered sugar

1 Tbsp vegan cream cheese

2 Tbsp canned coconut milk

Pinch sea salt

½ tsp vanilla

FOR THE GLAZE:

1. Whisk together the powdered sugar, cream cheese, coconut milk, sea salt, and vanilla until smooth.

2. Transfer the glaze to a small baggie (a Ziploc bag would suffice), cut off one corner, and squeeze the bag to drizzle over the donuts.

TO SERVE: Drizzle with glaze and indulge immediately (or freeze for a later date).

DESSERTS | 231

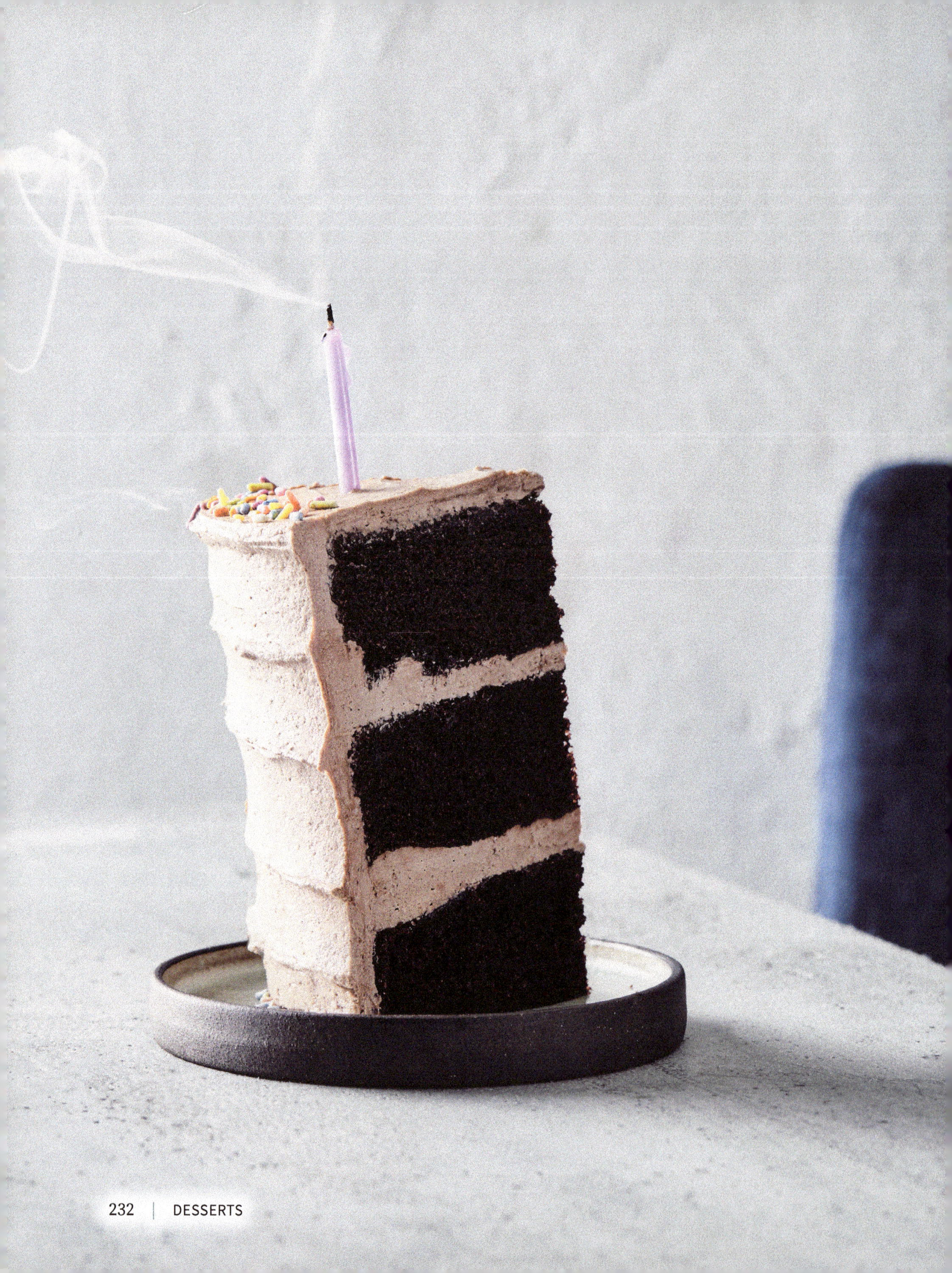

Magical Chocolate Birthday Cake

That feeling of blowing out the candles on your very own birthday cake, hoping what you wished for comes true, is simply magical. Say "Happy Birthday" to yourself or someone you love with this crowd-pleasing chocolate birthday cake!

PREP TIME: 15 minutes
BAKE TIME: 30 minutes
SERVINGS: 1 (6-inch) triple-layer cake or 18 cupcakes
SHELF LIFE: 1 month in the freezer

CAKE

1 Tbsp ground flax meal

3 Tbsp filtered water

2 cups gluten-free all-purpose flour

½ cup fair-trade organic cocoa

2 tsp baking powder

2 tsp baking soda

1 tsp sea salt

1 cup Sucanat (see note on page 221)

½ cup organic cane sugar

½ cup melted coconut oil or non-GMO canola oil

⅔ cup sweet potato puree

1 cup Coconut Milk (page 52)

2 tsp balsamic vinegar

1 Tbsp vanilla extract

FOR THE CAKE:

1. Preheat the oven to 350°F. Grease three 6-inch cake pans or line 18 cupcake cups with paper liners.

2. In a small bowl, combine the flax meal and the filtered water. Let sit for 5 minutes.

3. In a medium bowl, whisk together the flour, cocoa, baking powder, baking soda, and salt.

4. In a large bowl, using an electric hand mixer, combine the Sucanat, sugar, and oil. Add the sweet potato and mix again for 30 seconds. Add the coconut milk, balsamic vinegar, and vanilla and beat for 1 minute.

5. Add the thickened flax meal mixture into the sugar mixture and beat for 20 seconds.

6. Add the dry ingredients to the wet ingredients and mix with a hand mixer until the batter is smooth.

7. Divide the batter between the prepared cake pans or scoop into the cupcake liners.

8. Bake 25–30 minutes for the cakes on the center rack or 18 to 20 minutes for the cupcakes, until a knife comes out clean when you check it.

recipe continued

DESSERTS

FROSTING

¾ cup vegan shortening, softened (we use sustainable palm shortening)

½ cup vegan butter

3½ cups powdered sugar, sifted

¾ cup cocoa powder, sifted

2 Tbsp vanilla

2 Tbsp Coconut Milk (page 52)

Pinch sea salt

Colorful sprinkles, for garnish

FOR THE FROSTING:

1. In a large bowl, beat the vegan shortening and vegan butter until light and fluffy (about 2 to 3 minutes). Add the sifted powdered sugar, cocoa powder, and sea salt slowly and continue mixing until thick and creamy. Add the coconut milk a little at a time and mix until a consistency of smooth, spreadable frosting is achieved. Add more powdered sugar if the frosting gets too thin. Add the vanilla and beat for another minute or so.

TO SERVE: Allow the cakes or cupcakes to cool. Frost the cake, top with the sprinkles, and serve it up!

Strawberry Shortcake

Who doesn't love a good strawberry shortcake? Pair with a glass of white wine and a good movie on Netflix.... Now that sounds like the best evening!

PREP TIME: 10 minutes
BAKE TIME: 18–25 minutes
MAKES: about 1 (6-inch) triple-layer cake or 2 dozen cupcakes
SHELF LIFE: 1 month in the freezer

2 Tbsp chia seeds

6 Tbsp filtered water

2¼ cups gluten-free all-purpose flour

½ cup coconut flour

1½ tsp baking soda

1½ tsp baking powder

½ tsp xanthan gum

1 tsp sea salt

¾ cup vegan shortening, softened

1½ cups organic cane sugar

2¼ cups coconut yogurt

1 Tbsp vanilla extract

1 cup fresh strawberries, diced, and slightly mashed (plus more for garnish)

1 cup Whipped Cream (page 242)

1. Preheat the oven to 350°F. Lightly grease three 6-inch pans with shortening or line two 12-cup cupcake pans with liners.

2. In a small bowl, combine the chia seeds with the filtered water. Set aside.

3. In a medium bowl, whisk together the all-purpose flour, coconut flour, baking soda, baking powder, xanthan gum, and sea salt.

4. In a large bowl, cream the shortening, then add the cane sugar, yogurt, vanilla, and the chia seed mixture. Beat with a hand mixer until light and fluffy.

5. Add the dry ingredients to the wet ingredients and beat with an electric hand mixer. Gently fold the strawberries into the batter.

6. Divide the batter into the prepared cake pans or divide the batter among the cupcake liners.

7. Bake cake for 22 to 24 minutes and cupcakes for 18 minutes on the center rack, rotating pan(s) halfway through baking.

TO SERVE: Allow to cool completely before using a dollop of whipped cream and topping with fresh strawberries.

DESSERTS | 237

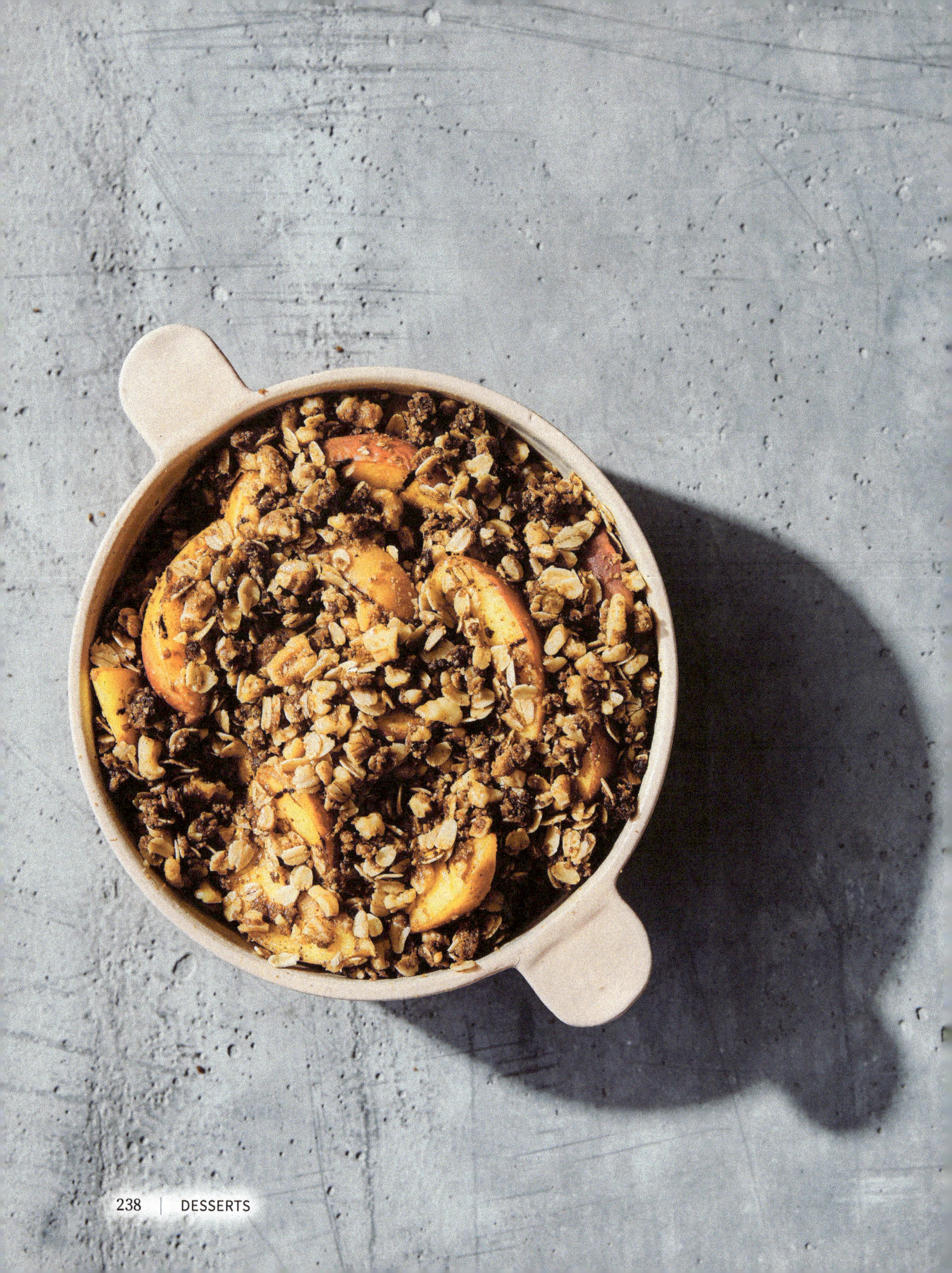

Summer Peach Crumble

This recipe makes us reminiscent of those warm summer nights, spending time with friends and family, and enjoying a delicious bowl of peach crumble. Top with your choice of vegan ice cream or our Raw Date Sauce (page 244). There are so many new ice creams to choose from now—like coconut milk, oat milk, and cashew milk ice cream.

PREP TIME: 10 minutes
BAKE TIME: 35 minutes
MAKES: one 8 x 8-inch loaf
SHELF LIFE: 3 days in the fridge

½ cup raw walnut pieces

¾ cup rolled oats

3 to 4 Tbsp Sucanat (see note on page 221)

2 Tbsp gluten-free all-purpose flour

1 tsp cinnamon

Pinch of sea salt

3 Tbsp cold vegan butter

1 Tbsp lemon juice

⅓ cup organic sugar

2 Tbsp arrowroot starch

4–6 peaches, sliced

Vegan ice cream, for serving (optional)

Raw Date Sauce (page 244), for serving (optional)

1. Preheat the oven to 350°F. Grease an 8 x 8-inch baking pan with a non-stick coconut oil spray.

2. In a medium bowl, combine the walnuts, oats, Sucanat, flour, cinnamon, and salt. Add the butter, and using your hands, crumble it into the mix until just combined. Set aside.

3. In a small bowl, add the lemon juice, sugar, and arrowroot starch. Add the peaches and toss until coated. Pour the peaches into the prepared pan. Top with the oat mixture. It will look crumbly.

4. Bake until golden brown and the center is bubbling (about 35 minutes). Let sit for 5 minutes before serving.

TO SERVE: This dessert is best served warm. Serve the peach crumble with a scoop of your favorite vegan ice cream or drizzle Raw Date Sauce over top.

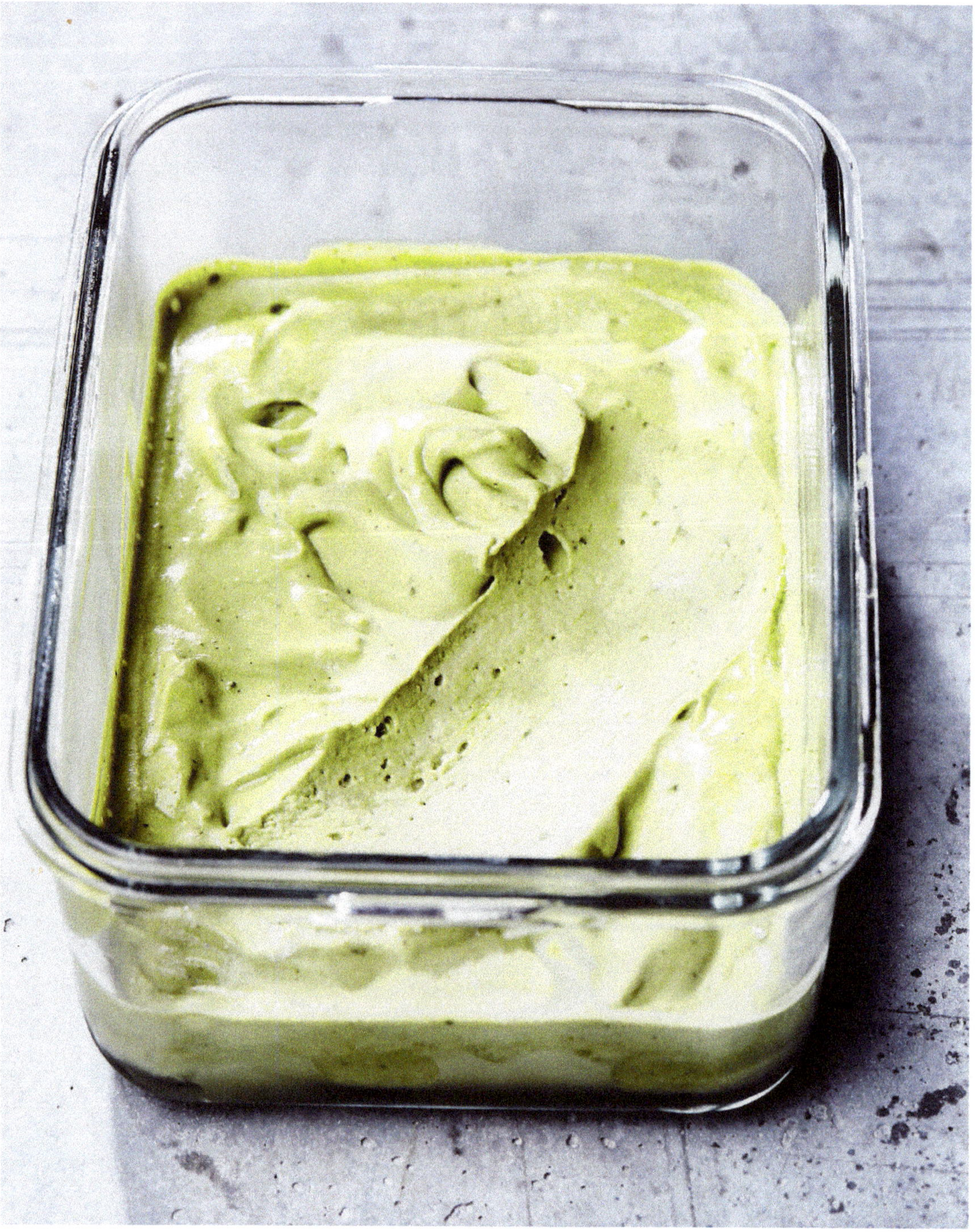

Matcha Nice Cream

We love matcha. We repeat: We LOVE Matcha! We try to have matcha at least once a day to give us a natural boost of caffeine and antioxidants (refer to Morning Matcha Recipe page 44). Who says you can't have nice cream for breakfast?! And when you can't, there's Kelly's Bake Shoppe lattes.

PREP TIME: 5 minutes
CHILL TIME: 30–45 min
MAKES: 4 servings

3–4 large frozen bananas, peeled, chopped
1 Tbsp of lemon juice
1 tsp maple syrup
1½ tsp matcha green tea powder

1. In a heavy-duty blender or food processor, blend all of the ingredients until smooth. Scrape down the sides as needed.

2. Pour into a glass container and freeze for about 30 minutes until firm.

TO SERVE: Enjoy on its own or as an addition to your favorite dessert (or breakfast … we're not judging).

NOTE: It's very important that your frozen bananas are chopped into medallions before blending. It will make the recipe much easier!

DESSERTS | 241

Whipped Cream

When we found out what incredible things we could do with chickpea water, we were so excited! We've made coconut whipped cream, quiche, cashew cream, and the list goes on. But nothing quite beats this amazing chickpea water (aquafaba) whipped cream. It's so light and fluffy and allergen friendly. Dollop it on some fresh fruit or on your favorite baked goods.

PREP TIME: 10 minutes
CHILL TIME: 20 minutes
MAKES: 1 cup
SHELF LIFE: 1 day

The liquid from a 15-oz can of chickpeas
⅛ tsp cream of tartar
1 Tbsp vanilla
2 Tbsp organic powdered sugar

1. Chill a glass bowl in the freezer for about 20 minutes.

2. Drain the chickpeas over the chilled large glass bowl in a colander and save the chickpea water. Move the chickpeas into a storage container and place them in the fridge to use another time (Crispy Baked Chickpeas 190).

3. Add the cream of tartar, vanilla, and sugar to the chickpea water. Using an electric hand mixer or a stand mixer fitted with the whip attachment on high speed, blend until stiff peaks begin to form (about 10 minutes). Trust us, they will begin to form, so just keep whipping!

TO SERVE: Use immediately or store in the fridge until needed.

Simple Vanilla Buttercream

This frosting is super easy. It is in our *Made With Love* cookbook, and we had to bring it back for a repeat performance because it is a staple in many homes. Get creative! You can make this into many flavors of frosting. To color or flavor this frosting, feel free to add your favorite natural food colors or natural extract flavors.

PREP TIME: 10 minutes
MAKES: enough to frost 24 cupcakes or one 6-inch triple-layer cake
SHELF LIFE: 3 days

1 cup vegan shortening, softened (we use sustainable palm shortening)
¼ cup vegan butter
4½ cups powdered sugar, sifted
2 Tbsp vanilla extract
2 Tbsp Coconut Milk (page 52) (optional)

1. In a large bowl, using an electric hand mixer or in a stand mixer fitted with the paddle attachment, blend the shortening with the butter for about 5 minutes, or until smooth and fluffy.

2. Slowly add the powdered sugar, ½ cup at a time, and continue to blend until the sugar is completely incorporated. Add the vanilla and beat well.

3. If the frosting is too stiff, add the coconut milk until the buttercream is the desired consistency. If you add too much milk and the buttercream is too soft, sprinkle in another Tbsp of powdered sugar.

TO SERVE: Use it to frost your favorite treat!

Raw Date Sauce

This is the perfect sauce for oatmeal porridge or waffles (page 119) or pancakes or ice cream or a piece of cake or a brownie…. You get the idea! It goes with everything!

PREP TIME: 5–7 minutes
SOAK TIME: 1 hour
MAKES: 1 cup
SHELF LIFE: 1 week in the fridge

¾ cup pitted dates
1 Tbsp coconut oil, melted
1 Tbsp coconut butter, melted
1 tsp vanilla extract
¼ tsp sea salt

1. In a medium bowl filled with 1½ cups of filtered water, add the dates and let sit for an hour. Do not discard water.

2. Add the dates and ¾ cup of the date water to a food processor or heavy-duty blender. Set the remaining ¾ cup water aside. Blend until smooth and add more date water as needed to make it a pourable sauce. You will need to scrape down sides and add more date water as needed.

3. Add the coconut oil, coconut butter, vanilla, and sea salt and blend again until very smooth. If it still feels too thick, just add a little more date water.

TO SERVE: Pour over your favorite recipe and use the leftover date water for your morning smoothie (page 75)!

DYK: Dates are rich in copper, magnesium, selenium, manganese and vitamin K. This makes for healthy bones! Why not do your best to give your body superstar status? Give up the junk food and opt for natural treats to enhance your only mode of transportation: your beautiful body.

Sugar-Free Frosting

This is our sugar-free frosting, aka our Skinny Frosting, which we use to sandwich our Skinny Cookies 2.0 (page 211). We could literally eat this frosting by the bowlful. Don't say we didn't warn you!

PREP TIME: 5 minutes
MAKES: 2½ cups
SHELF LIFE: 1 week in the fridge

1 cup vegan shortening, softened
1 cup cold vegan cream cheese
2 Tbsp vegan butter
¼ cup cocoa powder
¼ cup coconut milk powder
Pinch of cinnamon
½ cup maple syrup
2 Tbsp pure vanilla extract

1. In a small bowl and using an electric hand mixer, cream the shortening, cream cheese, and butter until smooth and fluffy (about 2 to 3 minutes).

2. Add the cocoa, coconut milk powder, and cinnamon, and beat again until smooth.

3. Add the maple syrup and vanilla and mix one last time with the hand mixer. Keep refrigerated until ready to use.

TO SERVE: Eat it straight from the bowl or sandwich two skinny cookies together for the ultimate guilt-free treat.

Cacao Sauce

Kelly discovered this treat of a recipe during her travels in Bali and recreated it for this book! It was served to her morning after morning on top of her dragon fruit granola. Crazy! It's so rich and delicious, you'll love every bite. Trust us, use it everywhere.

PREP TIME: 2 minutes
COOK TIME: 5 minutes
MAKES: about 1 cup
SHELF LIFE: 1 week in the fridge

½ cup cacao butter
¼ cup coconut butter
2 dates, softened and pitted
¼ cup cacao powder
¼ cup maple syrup

1. In a small saucepan over low heat, melt the cacao butter and coconut butter, stirring with a spatula.

2. Using a blender, blend the melted "butters" and the dates for 1 minute until smooth.

3. Add the cacao powder and maple syrup and blend once more for 20 seconds. Chill until ready to use.

TO SERVE: Drizzle this sauce on waffles, chia pudding, or eat it straight from the bowl. We're not judging!

NOTE: You can find cacao butter and coconut butter at most health-food stores.

Conclusion

Through it all, we're here to say, "Listen to your body."

If that means enjoying a plant-based meal one day a week or seven days a week, just do what feels right to you. Enjoy these recipes, have fun with them, and make them your own.

Remember this:

You are whole.
You are safe.
You are loved.
You are healthy.
You have the power to change your life.

We hope this book gives you what you came here for: delicious recipes and inspiration to become a healthier version of you. Good health and vibrant living are our inherent rights. It is time to give yourself permission to become your truest self.

Listen to your heart and listen to your body. Just do what feels right for you. Intuitively, we know what is best for our highest self.

In love and in eternal gratitude,

Kelly and Erinn
XO

Acknowledgements

We want to dedicate this book to all the loving souls in this world. We would not be here if we did not recognize and feel this loving energy within ourselves and this beautiful world.

Thank you to our publishers, at FriesenPress. Your attention to detail and superb quality is second to none. Not only do you provide incredible creative resources for authors to build out their perfect book but you also support freedom of speech, and that is something very near and dear to our hearts.

Thank you to our team at Kelly's Bake Shoppe for all you do, every darn day. Without you, there is no Kelly's Bake Shoppe. We truly love all of you.

From Erinn: Thank you to Michael, my rock, my love, and my best friend. Thank you for all you do for us every day. I love you.

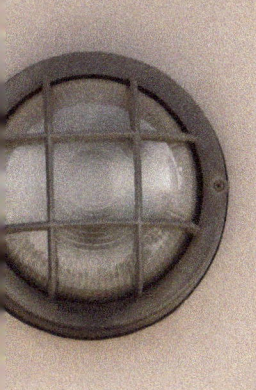

To each other... we're so grateful for one another and for always having each other's backs. To be the best of friends, and still somehow navigate the mom-daughter thing still brings the tears of gratitude for all we have created and worked so hard for. The love runs through eternity.

To our animals, Yukon, George (Mr. Pills), Daisy, Petunia (Tuna Fish), and the late, precious, Zoe, who continues to teach us love, consciousness, and forgiveness daily, thank you for reminding us that there is only the present moment.

Love Kelly & Erinn.

From Kelly: May my heart expand into more love and hold space for my soul's journey and all I need to learn and evolve and grow into. I am reminded that through all the experiences in my life, I am always divinely guided and protected. I am love. We are love. Each and every one of us is love. It is all we are. May we all find the courage and bravery to expand even more into all we are meant to be... and so it is.

About the Authors

Kelly Childs lives north of the Greater Toronto Area with her fur babies growing dahlias and creating her art. Erinn Weatherbie, her husband Michael, and their shepherd Yukon live close by in this nature wonderland. You can learn more about their story, philosophy, and bakery at: www.kellysxo.com

Additional Resources

"Almonds | The Nutrition Source | Harvard T.H. Chan School of Public Health." *Harvard T.H. Chan School of Public Health*, https://www.hsph.harvard.edu/nutritionsource/food-features/almonds/.

Chin, Kim. "6 Benefits of Apple Cider Vinegar." *Healthline*, 2021, https://www.healthline.com/nutrition/6-proven-health-benefits-of-apple-cider-vinegar.

McDonough, Darcy, and Cording, Jessica. "Apple Cider Vinegar: Benefits, The Mother, Safety & Use | mindbodygreen." *MindBodyGreen*, 2020, https://www.mindbodygreen.com/articles/apple-cider-vinegar-benefits.

"What are Adaptogens & Types." *Cleveland Clinic*, 2022, https://my.clevelandclinic.org/health/drugs/22361-adaptogens.

Marengo, Katherine. "12 health benefits of avocado." *Medical News Today*, 2023, https://www.medicalnewstoday.com/articles/270406.

Mikstas, Christine. "Health Benefits of Barley Grass." *WebMD*, 2022, https://www.webmd.com/diet/health-benefits-barley-grass.

Raman, Ryan, and Alan Carter. "Top 11 Health Benefits of Bee Pollen." *Healthline*, 2018, https://www.healthline.com/nutrition/bee-pollen.

Naturally, Renée. "The Health Benefits of Cacao." *Family Health Diary*, 2016, https://www.familyhealthdiary.co.nz/the-health-benefits-of-cacao/.

Nagdeve, Meenakshi. "14 Evidence Based Benefits of Chia Seeds." *Organic Facts*, 2020, https://www.organicfacts.net/health-benefits/seed-and-nut/health-benefits-of-chia-seeds.html

Axe, Josh. "Coconut Butter Nutrition Facts, Benefits and How to Make." *Dr. Axe*, 2017, https://draxe.com/nutrition/coconut-butter/.

Spritzler, Franziska, and Jillian Kubala. "Coconut Milk: Health Benefits and Uses - Nutrition." *Healthline*, 2018, https://www.healthline.com/nutrition/coconut-milk.

Axe, Josh. "Coconut Oil Benefits, Nutrition and Popular Uses." *Dr. Axe*, 2022, https://draxe.com/nutrition/coconut-oil-benefits/.

Bandara, Sajini. "Benefits of coconut oil." *LiveLife*, 2021, https://livelife.lk/2021/11/30/benefits-of-coconut-oil/.

"Breast Milk & Monolaurin — Monolaurin and More." *Monolaurin and More*, 2020, https://www.monolaurinandmore.com/articles/breast-milk-and-monolaurin.

Magee, Elaine. "Flaxseed Health Benefits, Food Sources, Recipes, and Tips for Using It." *WebMD*, https://www.webmd.com/diet/features/benefits-of-flaxseed.

"Plant Sources of Omega-3s." *Cleveland Clinic*, 2019, https://my.clevelandclinic.org/health/articles/17651-plant-sources-of-omega-3s.

Marengo, Katherine. "9 benefits of hemp seeds: Nutrition, health, and use." *Medical News Today*, 2018, https://www.medicalnewstoday.com/articles/323037#_noHeaderPrefixedContent.

West, Helen. "6 Evidence-Based Health Benefits of Lemons - Nutrition." *Healthline*, 2019, https://www.healthline.com/nutrition/6-lemon-health-benefits.

"Lemon balm Information." *Mount Sinai*, https://www.mountsinai.org/health-library/herb/lemon-balm.

"Health Benefits of Honey – Medcom Personnel." *Medcom Personnel*, 2017, https://www.medcompersonnel.co.uk/health-benefits-of-honey/.

Saling, Joseph. "Manuka Honey: Medicinal Uses, Benefits, and Side Effects." *WebMD*, 2021, https://www.webmd.com/a-to-z-guides/manuka-honey-medicinal-uses.

Link, Rachael. "Maca Root Benefits, Nutrition, Dosage and Side Effects." *Dr. Axe*, 2022, https://draxe.com/nutrition/maca-root-benefits/.

Thambinayagam, Kevin. "MATCHA THE GREEN TEAS FAR BEHIND? EVERYTHING ABOUT THIS GREEN TEA." *Olinda Teas*, https://olindateas.com/blogs/news/is-matcha-putting-other-green-teas-far-behind-everything-about-this-type-of-green-tea.

"The Benefits of Cordyceps and Lion's Mane Together." *Rritual Superfoods*, 2021, https://rritual.com/blogs/health/the-benefits-of-cordyceps-and-lion-s-mane-together.

"Health Benefits of Spirulina." *Natural Foods Plus*, https://www.naturalfoodsplus.com/health-is-wealth-blog/health-benefits-of-spirulina.

McCulloch, Marsha. "Sunflower Seeds: Nutrition, Health Benefits and How to Eat Them." *Healthline*, 2023, https://www.healthline.com/nutrition/sunflower-seeds.

Link, Rachael. "Sesame Seeds Benefits, Nutrition, Allergy, Side Effects." *Dr. Axe*, 2023, https://draxe.com/nutrition/sesame-seeds/.

"Health Benefits of Wild Blueberries." *Wild Blueberries*, https://www.wildblueberries.com/health-benefits/.

"Benefits and Side Effects of Turmeric." *Facty*, https://facty.com/food/nutrition/10-benefits-of-turmeric/?style=quick&utm_source=adwords-ca&adid=490388750538&ad_group_id=89726240343&utm_medium=c-search&utm_term=health%20benefits%20of%20turmeric&utm_campaign=FH-CA-Search-10-Benefits-of-Turmeric-Desktop&g.

"What is Pine Needle Tea? And What is it Good For?" *Dynasty of Tea*, 2022, https://thedynastyoftea.com/allblogs/what-is-pine-needle-tea.

"10 Reasons You Should Be Drinking Pine Needle Tea." *Forest Holidays*, https://www.forestholidays.co.uk/forestipedia/10-reasons-you-should-be-drinking-pine-needle-tea/.

Axe, Josh. "How to Boost Your Immune System: 19 Boosters." *Dr. Axe*, 7 February 2023, https://draxe.com/health/how-to-boost-your-immune-system/.

Pitura, Paul. "Blue Zone Costa Rica: Living Longer, Living Better - Special Places CR." *Special Places of Costa Rica*, 2021, https://www.specialplacesofcostarica.com/blue-zone-costa-rica-living-longer-living-better/

"Top 7 Plant-Based Sources of Healthy Fats." *Vibrant Vegan*, 11 August 2021, https://vibrantvegan.co.uk/blogs/news/top-7-plant-based-sources-of-healthy-fats.

Richter, Amy. "7 Proven Health Benefits of Brazil Nuts." *Healthline*, 2023, https://www.healthline.com/nutrition/brazil-nuts-benefits.

Richter, Amy. "8 Proven Health Benefits of Dates - Nutrition." *Healthline*, 2022, https://www.healthline.com/nutrition/benefits-of-dates.

Index

Page numbers in *italics* refer to photos.

A

activated charcoal, in Black Lemonade, *58*, 59
adaptogens, 20, *72–73*
almond butter
    Almond Ginger Dressing, 196
    Almond Maca Butter, 108, *109*
    Compost Cookies, 213
    Golden Mylkshake, 79
    Green Goddess Smoothie Bowl, *90*, 91
    Skinny Cookie 2.0, *210*, 211
    Sweet Potato Toasts, 108, *109*
Almond Ginger Dressing, 196
almond meal, in "Can't Handle this Jelly" Muffins, *222*, 223–224
almonds
    about, 20, *128*
    Banana Bread Superfood Granola, 96, *97*
    Chopped Kale Power Salad, *136*, 137
    Fat Bombs, *114*, 115
    Kelly and Erinn's Superfood Raw-Nola, 100, *101*
    Kelp Noodle Salad with Almond Ginger Dressing, 138, *139*
    Skinny Cookie 2.0, *210*, 211
apple cider vinegar
    about, 20
    Wellness Shot, 68, *69*
apple sauce, *201*
apples

Palm Springs Smoothie, 86, *87*
    Simple Green, *62*, 63
aquafaba, in Whipped Cream, 242
ashwagandha
    about, 20, 44, *73*
    Hormone Balancing Smoothie, 80
    Kelly + Erinn's Morning Matcha, 44, *45*
    Kelly and Erinn's Superfood Raw-Nola, 100, *101*
avocados
    about, 20–21, *129*
    Avocado Lime Topping, 108, *109*
    B.L.A.T. Sandwich, 166, *167*
    Buddha Bowl 2.0, *132*, 133
    Chopped Kale Power Salad, *136*, 137
    Friday Night Dip, *184*, 185
    Guac and Chips, *180*, 181
    Hormone Balancing Smoothie, 80
    Kelp Noodle Salad with Almond Ginger Dressing, 138, *139*
    Mermaid Bowl, 92, *93*
    Pura Vida Smoothie, 81
    Savory Breakfast Bowl, *122*, 123
    Sweet Potato Smoothie, *84*, 85
    Sweet Potato Toasts, 108, *109*
    Toasts with Avocado, 124, *125–126*, 127
awareness, 12

B

baked goods, creating gluten-free, 3–4
baking ingredients, pantry essentials, 32, *200–201*
baking sheets, 36

bananas
    Banana Bread Superfood Granola, 96, *97*
    Best Banana Bread, 220

Choco Bowl, *98*, 99
Date Shake, 76, *77*
Golden Mylkshake, 79
Green Goddess Smoothie Bowl, *90*, 91
Hormone Balancing Smoothie, 80
Matcha Nice Cream, *240*, 241
Mermaid Bowl, 92, *93*
Palm Springs Smoothie, 86, *87*
Pura Vida Smoothie, 81
Skinny Cookie 2.0, *210*, 211
Sunrise Smoothie, 82, *83*
Sweet Potato Smoothie, *84*, 85
barley grass powder, 21
basil
   about, 21
   Classic Pesto, 190
   Simple Green, *62*, 63
   Toasts with Avocado, *126*, 127
   Triple Goddess Soup, *150*, 151
bean sprouts, in Pad Thai, 152, *153*
bee pollen, 21
beets
   Quick and Easy Pickled Vegetables, 186
   Roasted Beet Hummus, *192*, 193
   Street Beet Burger, *130*, 162–163, *163*
   Sunrise Smoothie, 82, *83*
bell peppers
   Cauliflower Pizza, *154*, 155–156
   Quick and Easy Pickled Vegetables, 186
Best Banana Bread, 220
Best Vegan Mayo, 197
beverages
   Black Lemonade, *58*, 59
   Cashew Milk, 53
   Celery Juice, 64
   Chia Agua Fresca, 60, *61*
   Coconut Milk, 52
   Detox Juice, 54, *55*
   Digestive Tincture, 56–57, *57*
   Kelly + Erinn's Morning Matcha, 44, *45*
   Oat Milk, 51
   Simple Green, *62*, 63
   Soul-Soothing Turmeric Tonic, *56*, 66, 67
   Supernatural Cacao "Coffee," 48, *49*
   Wake-Up Tonic, 47
   Wellness Shot, 68, *69*
   White Pine Needle Tea, *56*, 71
   See also smoothies
Birthday Cake, Magical Chocolate, *232*, 233, 235
black beans
   refried, in Friday Night Dip, *184*, 185
   Street Beet Burger, *130*, 162–163, *163*
Black Lemonade, *58*, 59
black pepper, 89
B.L.A.T. Sandwich, 166, *167*
blenders, 36
Blue Majik, 92
Blue Zones, 81
blueberries, dried, in Chopped Kale Power Salad, *136*, 137
blueberries, wild
   about, 28
   Wild Blueberry Chia Jam, *110*, 111
boundaries, 16
Brazil nuts
   about, *129*, 198
   Our Famous Brazil Nut Parmesan, 198
bread
   Best Banana Bread, 220
   Toasts with Avocado, 124, *125–126*, 127
breakfast
   Banana Bread Superfood Granola, 96, *97*
   Choco Bowl, *98*, 99
   Coconut Yogurt, 112
   Creamsicle Clementine Chia Pudding, 104, *105*
   Fat Bombs, *114*, 115
   Kelly and Erinn's Superfood Raw-Nola, 100, *101*
   Lemon "Cheesecake" Chia Pudding, *106*, 107
   Pumpkin Waffles, *118*, 119–120
   Raspberry Cloud Chia Pudding, 116
   Savory Breakfast Bowl, *122*, 123
   Sweet Potato Porridge, 103
   Sweet Potato Toasts, 108, *109*
   Toasts with Avocado, 124, *125–126*, 127
   Wild Blueberry Chia Jam, *110*, 111
breakfast bowls
   Choco Bowl, *98*, 99
   Savory Breakfast Bowl, *122*, 123
broccoli

Cauliflower Steaks with Cashew Butter Kimchi Sauce and Grilled Rapini, 169–170
Curly Green Bowl, 134, *135*
Triple Goddess Soup, *150*, 151
broccoli rabe, in Cauliflower Steaks with Cashew Butter Kimchi Sauce and Grilled Rapini, 169–170, *171*
Broth, Gut Healing, *144*, 145
brown rice syrup, *200*
brownies, creating gluten-free, 4
brussels sprouts, in Loaded Lentil Salad, *140*, 141

C

cabbage, in Gut Healing Broth, *144*, 145
cacao
    about, 21–22, *40*, 99
    Cacao Sauce, 246
    Choco Bowl, *98*, 99
    Supernatural Cacao "Coffee," 48, *49*
cacao butter, in Cacao Sauce, 246
cacao nibs
    about, 22
    Fat Bombs, *114*, 115
caffeine, 44
Cake, Magical Chocolate Birthday, *232*, 233, 235
cane sugar, *201*
canned goods, pantry essentials, 32
cannellini beans, in Toasts with Avocado, *126*, 127
canning jars, 36
"Can't Handle this Jelly" Muffins, *222*, 223–224
carrot juice
    Pad Thai, 152, *153*
    Sunrise Smoothie, 82, *83*
carrots
    B.L.A.T. Sandwich, 166, *167*
    Carrot Bacon, 174, *175*
    Detox Juice, 54, *55*
    Easy Cheese Sauce, 194
    Eternal Glow Bowl, 88, *89*
    Gut Healing Broth, *144*, 145
    Pad Thai, 152, *153*
    Quick and Easy Pickled Vegetables, 186
    Warming Squash and Carrot Soup, 146, *147*
cashew butter
    Chocolate Chunk Turmeric Cookies, *218*, 219
    Skinny Cookie 2.0, *210*, 211

buckwheat groats, in Choco Bowl, *98*, 99
Buddha Bowl 2.0, *132*, 133
Burger, Street Beet, *130*, 162–163, *163*
business, living with consciousness, 12, 15–16
Buttercream Frosting, 243
butternut squash
    Eternal Glow Bowl, 88, *89*
    Warming Squash and Carrot Soup, 146, *147*
butters, pantry essentials, 33

Cashew Milk, recipe, 53
cashews
    Cashew Milk, 53
    Cauliflower Steaks with Cashew Butter Kimchi Sauce and Grilled Rapini, *168*, 169–170, *171*
    Easy Cheese Sauce, 194
    Eazy Cheezy Kale Chips, *176*, 177
    Fat Bombs, *114*, 115
    Kimchi Cashew Butter Sauce, *168*, 170, *171*
    Lemon "Cheesecake" Chia Pudding, *106*, 107
    Pad Thai, 152, *153*
cauliflower
    Cauliflower Pizza, *154*, 155–156
    Cauliflower Steaks with Cashew Butter Kimchi Sauce and Grilled Rapini, *168*, 169–170, *171*
    Movie Night Popcorn, 182, *183*
    Quick and Easy Pickled Vegetables, 186
    Warm Cauliflower Salad, 142, *143*
cayenne, 48
celery
    about, 64
    Celery Juice, 64
    Gut Healing Broth, *144*, 145
    Simple Green, *62*, 63
chaga mushrooms, 27
challenges, 15–16
chard, in Buddha Bowl 2.0, *132*, 133
Cheese Sauce, Easy, 194
"Cheesecake" Chia Pudding, Lemon, *106*, 107
Cheezy Kale Chips, Eazy, *176*, 177
chia pudding
    Creamsicle Clementine Chia Pudding, 104, *105*
    Lemon "Cheesecake" Chia Pudding, *106*, 107

Raspberry Cloud Chia Pudding, 116
chia seeds
   about, 22, 60
   Banana Bread Superfood Granola, 96, *97*
   "Can't Handle this Jelly" Muffins, *222*, 223–224
   Chia Agua Fresca, 60, *61*
   Chocolate-Dipped Macaroons, 228
   Compost Cookies, 213
   Creamsicle Clementine Chia Pudding, 104, *105*
   egg replacement, 22, 32, *201*
   Golden Mylkshake, 79
   Kelly and Erinn's Superfood Raw-Nola, 100, *101*
   Lemon "Cheesecake" Chia Pudding, *106*, 107
   Raspberry Cloud Chia Pudding, 116
   Strawberry Shortcake, 236, *237*
   Street Beet Burger, *130*, 162–163, *163*
   Wild Blueberry Chia Jam, *110*, 111
chickpeas
   Chopped Kale Power Salad, *136*, 137
   Crispy Baked Chickpeas, 178, *179*
   Roasted Beet Hummus, *192*, 193
   Whipped Cream, 242
chicory root powder, in Supernatural Cacao "Coffee," 48, *49*
Chips, Eazy Cheezy Kale, *176*, 177
Choco Bowl, *98*, 99
chocolate
   about, *40*
   Chocolate Chunk Turmeric Cookies, *218*, 219
   Magical Chocolate Birthday Cake, *232*, 233, 235
chocolate chips
   about, *201*
   Banana Bread Superfood Granola, 96, *97*
   Best Banana Bread, 220
   Compost Cookies, 213
   Indulgent Shortbread Cookies, 214, *215*
   Skinny Cookie 2.0, *210*, 211
Chocolate-Dipped Macaroons, 228
Chopped Kale Power Salad, *136*, 137
cilantro
   about, 22
   Kelp Noodle Salad with Almond Ginger Dressing, 138, *139*
   Simple Green, *62*, 63

Cinnamon Bun Donuts, 229–230, *231*
Classic Pesto, 190
Clementine Chia Pudding, Creamsicle, 104, *105*
cocoa
   Magical Chocolate Birthday Cake, *232*, 233, 235
   Sugar-Free Frosting, 245
coconut, shredded
   "Can't Handle this Jelly" Muffins, *222*, 223–224
   Chocolate-Dipped Macaroons, 228
   Coconut Milk, 52
   Compost Cookies, 213
   Creamsicle Clementine Chia Pudding, 104, *105*
   Fat Bombs, *114*, 115
   Golden Mylkshake, 79
   Kelly and Erinn's Superfood Raw-Nola, 100, *101*
   Skinny Cookie 2.0, *210*, 211
coconut butter
   about, 22
   Cacao Sauce, 246
   Fat Bombs, *114*, 115
   Kelly + Erinn's Morning Matcha, 44, *45*
   Raw Date Sauce, 244
coconut milk
   about, 22–23
   Coconut Yogurt, 112
   recipe, 52
coconut oil, 23, 48, *128*
coconut water
   Palm Springs Smoothie, 86, *87*
   Pura Vida Smoothie, 81
Coconut Yogurt, 112
Compost Cookies, 213
condiments, pantry essentials, 32
conscious life and business, 12, 15–16
cookies
   Chocolate Chunk Turmeric Cookies, *218*, 219
   Chocolate-Dipped Macaroons, 228
   Compost Cookies, 213
   Ginger Molasses Cookies, 212
   Indulgent Shortbread Cookies, 214, *215*
   Lemony Shortbread Cookies, 214
   Matcha Shortbread, *216*, 217
   Skinny Cookie 2.0, *210*, 211
   Sugar Cookies with Pumpkin Frosting, *204*, 205–206

cordyceps mushrooms
    about, 27, 46, *72*
    Golden Mylkshake, 79
    Wake-Up Tonic, 47
corn, in Sweet Roasted Corn Soup, *148*, 149
corn tortillas, in Savory Breakfast Bowl, *122*, 123
cornmeal, in Creamy Polenta with Oven-Roasted Tomatoes, Kale, and Mushrooms, 158, *159*
Costa Rica, 81
cranberries, dried, in Skinny Cookie 2.0, *210*, 211
cream cheese
    Cinnamon Bun Donuts glaze, 230, *231*
    Sugar-Free Frosting, 245

Creamsicle Clementine Chia Pudding, 104, *105*
Creamy Polenta with Oven-Roasted Tomatoes, Kale, and Mushrooms, 158, *159*
Creamy Pumpkin Mac 'n' Cheese, *160*, 161
Crispy Baked Chickpeas, 178, *179*
Crumble, Summer Peach, *238*, 239
cucumber, in Quick and Easy Pickled Vegetables, 186
Cupcakes, S'mores, *226*, 227
curcumin, about, 28, 41
    See also turmeric
Curly Green Bowl, 134, *135*

D

dates
    about, 244
    Cacao Sauce, 246
    Coconut Milk, 52
    Date Shake, 76, *77*
    Fat Bombs, *114*, 115
    Kelly and Erinn's Superfood Raw-Nola, 100, *101*
    Oat Milk, 51
    Raw Date Sauce, 244
desserts
    Best Banana Bread, 220
    Cacao Sauce, 246
    "Can't Handle this Jelly" Muffins, *222*, 223–224
    Chocolate Chunk Turmeric Cookies, *218*, 219
    Chocolate-Dipped Macaroons, 228
    Cinnamon Bun Donuts, 229–230, *231*
    Compost Cookies, 213
    Ginger Molasses Cookies, 212
    Indulgent Shortbread Cookies, 214, *215*
    Magical Chocolate Birthday Cake, *232*, 233, 235
    Manuka Honey Baked Figs, *208*, 209
    Matcha Nice Cream, *240*, 241
    Matcha Shortbread, *216*, 217

    Raw Date Sauce, 244
    Simple Vanilla Buttercream, 243
    Skinny Cookie 2.0, *210*, 211
    S'mores Cupcakes, *226*, 227
    Strawberry Shortcake, 236, *237*
    Sugar Cookies with Pumpkin Frosting, *204*, 205–206
    Sugar-Free Frosting, 245
    Summer Peach Crumble, *238*, 239
    Whipped Cream, 242
Detox Juice, 54, *55*
diet, life stages and, 19
Digestive Tincture, 56–57, *57*
dinosaur kale, in Chopped Kale Power Salad, *136*, 137
dips
    Friday Night Dip, *184*, 185
    Guac and Chips, *180*, 181
Donuts, Cinnamon Bun, 229–230, *231*
dressings
    Almond Ginger Dressing, 196
    Lemon Tahini Dressing, 197
drinks. *See* beverages; smoothies
dry goods, pantry essentials, 32

E

Easy Cheese Sauce, 194
Eazy Cheezy Kale Chips, *176*, 177
echinacea, in Soul-Soothing Turmeric Tonic, 56, 66, 67
egg replacements, 22, 32, *201*
electric mixers, 36

entrees
    B.L.A.T. Sandwich, 166, *167*
    Buddha Bowl 2.0, *132*, 133
    Cauliflower Pizza, *154*, 155–156

Cauliflower Steaks with Cashew Butter Kimchi Sauce and Grilled Rapini, *168*, 169–170, *171*
Chopped Kale Power Salad, *136*, 137
Creamy Polenta with Oven-Roasted Tomatoes, Kale, and Mushrooms, 158, *159*
Creamy Pumpkin Mac 'n' Cheese, *160*, 161
Curly Green Bowl, 134, *135*
Gut Healing Broth, *144*, 145
Kelp Noodle Salad with Almond Ginger Dressing, 138, *139*
Loaded Lentil Salad, *140*, 141
Pad Thai, 152–153, *153*
Street Beet Burger, *130*, 162–163, *163*
Sweet Potato Nachos, *164*, 165
Sweet Roasted Corn Soup, *148*, 149
Triple Goddess Soup, *150*, 151
Warm Cauliflower Salad, 142, *143*
Warming Squash and Carrot Soup, 146, *147*
Eternal Glow Bowl, 88, *89*
eye health, 88

F

Fat Bombs, *114*, 115
fats
   in avocado, 127
   importance of, 20–21, 115, *128–129*
   pantry essentials, 31–32
   plant-based, 23
Figs, Manuka Honey Baked, *208*, 209
flaxseed
   about, 25
   Banana Bread Superfood Granola, 96, *97*
   "Can't Handle this Jelly" Muffins, *222*, 223–224
   Cauliflower Pizza, *154*, 155–156
   egg replacement, 32
   Ginger Molasses Cookies, 212
   Kelly and Erinn's Superfood Raw-Nola, 100, *101*
   Pumpkin Waffles, *118*, 119–120
   Street Beet Burger, *130*, 162–163, *163*
flour, gluten-free, *200*
food
   quality of, 19
   where to buy, 31
food processors, 36
French lentils, in Loaded Lentil Salad, *140*, 141
Friday Night Dip, *184*, 185
frosting
   Magical Chocolate Birthday Cake, *232*, 235
   Pumpkin Frosting, 206, *207*
   Simple Vanilla Buttercream, 243
   Sugar-Free Frosting, 245
fruit jam
   "Can't Handle this Jelly" Muffins, *222*, 223–224
   Wild Blueberry Chia Jam, *110*, 111
fruits, pantry essentials, 33

G

garlic
   about, *41*
   Gut Healing Broth, *144*, 145
ginger
   about, 25, *41*
   Almond Ginger Dressing, 196
   Detox Juice, 54, *55*
   Digestive Tincture, 57, *57*
   Eternal Glow Bowl, 88, *89*
   Gut Healing Broth, *144*, 145
   Palm Springs Smoothie, 86, *87*
   Soul-Soothing Turmeric Tonic, *56*, *66*, 67
   Sunrise Smoothie, 82, *83*
   Wellness Shot, 68, *69*
Ginger Molasses Cookies, 212
gluten-free baked goods, challenges of, 3–4
Golden Mylkshake, 79
Grail Springs Retreat Centre, 116, 151
grains, pantry essentials, 31
granola
   Banana Bread Superfood Granola, 96, *97*
   Kelly and Erinn's Superfood Raw-Nola, 100, *101*
grapefruit
   about, *40*
   Detox Juice, 54, *55*
   Wake-Up Tonic, 47

green beans, in Quick and Easy Pickled Vegetables, 186
Green Goddess Smoothie Bowl, *90*, 91
grocery list, 31–33

H

hemp seeds
    about, 25
    Fat Bombs, *114*, 115
    Kelly and Erinn's Superfood Raw-Nola, 100, *101*
    Skinny Cookie 2.0, *210*, 211
    Supernatural Cacao "Coffee," 48, *49*
    Toasts with Avocado, 124, *125*
herbs, pantry essentials, 32, 33

I

ice cream scoops, 36
immunity boosters, *40–41*

J

jackfruit, in Sweet Potato Nachos, *164*, 165
jam
    "Can't Handle this Jelly" Muffins, *222*, 223–224
    Wild Blueberry Chia Jam, *110*, 111
jarred goods, pantry essentials, 32
juice
    Black Lemonade, *58*, 59

K

kale
    about, 123
    Buddha Bowl 2.0, *132*, 133
    Chopped Kale Power Salad, *136*, 137
    Creamy Polenta with Oven-Roasted Tomatoes, Kale, and Mushrooms, 158, *159*
    Eazy Cheezy Kale Chips, *176*, 177
    Gut Healing Broth, *144*, 145
    Pad Thai, 152, *153*
    Palm Springs Smoothie, 86, *87*
    Savory Breakfast Bowl, *122*, 123
    Simple Green, *62*, 63
Kelly + Erinn's Morning Matcha, 44, *45*

L

leafy greens
    about, 63

Guac and Chips, *180*, 181
Gut Healing Broth, *144*, 145

honey
    about, 21, 26
    Manuka Honey Baked Figs, *208*, 209
Hormone Balancing Smoothie, 80
hummus
    Roasted Beet Hummus, *192*, 193
    Toasts with Avocado, *126*, 127

Indulgent Shortbread Cookies, 214, *215*

    Celery Juice, 64
    Chia Agua Fresca, 60, *61*
    Detox Juice, 54, *55*
    Simple Green, *62*, 63
juicers, 36

Kelly and Erinn's Superfood Raw-Nola, 100, *101*
Kelly's Bake Shoppe, 7, 15
kelp noodles
    about, 25
    Kelp Noodle Salad with Almond Ginger Dressing, 138, *139*
Kimchi Cashew Butter Sauce, *168*, 170, *171*
Kindfood, 3, 15, 133
kitchen tools, 36
kiwis
    Green Goddess Smoothie Bowl, *90*, 91
    Mermaid Bowl, 92, *93*
knives, 36
kombucha, 33

    Buddha Bowl 2.0, *132*, 133
    Gut Healing Broth, *144*, 145

leeks, in Gut Healing Broth, *144*, 145
legumes, pantry essentials, 31
lemon balm
    about, 25–26, *56*
    Digestive Tincture, 57, *57*
lemons
    about, 25
    Black Lemonade, *58*, 59
    Digestive Tincture, 57, *57*
    Lemon "Cheesecake" Chia Pudding, *106*, 107
    Lemon Tahini Dressing, 197
    Lemony Shortbread Cookies, 214
    Soul-Soothing Turmeric Tonic, *56*, *66*, 67
    Wake-Up Tonic, 47
    Wellness Shot, 68, *69*

M

Mac 'n' Cheese, Creamy Pumpkin, *160*, 161
maca
    about, 26, *73*
    Almond Maca Butter, 108
    Banana Bread Superfood Granola, 96, *97*
    Hormone Balancing Smoothie, 80
    Kelly and Erinn's Superfood Raw-Nola, 100, *101*
    Sweet Potato Toasts, 108, *109*
Macaroons, Chocolate-Dipped, 228
Magical Chocolate Birthday Cake, *232*, 233, 235
mangoes, in Eternal Glow Bowl, 88, *89*
Manuka honey
    about, 26
    Manuka Honey Baked Figs, *208*, 209
maple syrup, *201*
marshmallows, in S'mores Cupcakes, *226*, 227
matcha
    about, 26, *41*, 44
    Kelly + Erinn's Morning Matcha, 44, *45*
    Matcha Nice Cream, *240*, 241
    Matcha Shortbread, *216*, 217
Mayo, Best Vegan, 197
medicinal mushrooms, 26–27
    See also individual mushrooms
meditation, 12, 15
medjool dates
    Date Shake, 76, *77*
    Fat Bombs, *114*, 115

lentils
    Loaded Lentil Salad, *140*, 141
    Savory Breakfast Bowl, *122*, 123
life, living with consciousness, 12, 15–16
limes
    Avocado Lime Topping, 108, *109*
    Chia Agua Fresca, 60, *61*
    Sweet Potato Toasts, 108, *109*
lion's mane mushrooms
    about, 27, 46
    Hormone Balancing Smoothie, 80
    Wake-Up Tonic, 47
Loaded Lentil Salad, *140*, 141
love, 16

Mermaid Bowl, 92, *93*
milks, plant-based
    Cashew Milk, 53
    Coconut Milk, 52
    Oat Milk, 51
    pantry essentials, 33
milkshakes
    Date Shake, 76, *77*
    Golden Mylkshake, 79
mint
    Chia Agua Fresca, 60, *61*
    Digestive Tincture, 57, *57*
    Kelp Noodle Salad with Almond Ginger Dressing, 138, *139*
    Palm Springs Smoothie, 86, *87*
    Simple Green, *62*, 63
miso
    Gut Healing Broth, *144*, 145
    Turmeric Miso Sauce, 196
Molasses, Ginger Cookies, 212
moringa powder, *72*
Movie Night Popcorn, 182, *183*
Muffins, "Can't Handle this Jelly," *222*, 223–224
mushrooms
    Cauliflower Pizza, *154*, 155–156
    Creamy Polenta with Oven-Roasted Tomatoes, Kale, and Mushrooms, 158, *159*
    Gut Healing Broth, *144*, 145

medicinal, 26–27
Savory Breakfast Bowl, *122*, 123

N

Nachos, Sweet Potato, *164*, 165
Nice Cream, Matcha, *240*, 241
noise, 12
noodles, in Pad Thai, 152, *153*

O

Oat Milk, recipe, 51
oats
    about, 27
    Banana Bread Superfood Granola, 96, *97*
    "Can't Handle this Jelly" Muffins, *222*, 223–224
    Chocolate Chunk Turmeric Cookies, *218*, 219
    Compost Cookies, 213
    Kelly and Erinn's Superfood Raw-Nola, 100, *101*
    Oat Milk, 51
    Savory Breakfast Bowl, *122*, 123
    Skinny Cookie 2.0, *210*, 211

P

Pad Thai, 152–153, *153*
Palm Springs Smoothie, 86, *87*
pantry
    essentials, 31–33
    superfoods, 20–28
papayas, in Sunrise Smoothie, 82, *83*
Parmesan, Our Famous Brazil Nut, 198
pastas
    Creamy Pumpkin Mac 'n' Cheese, *160*, 161
    pantry essentials, 31
Peach Crumble, Summer, *238*, 239
peanut butter
    Pad Thai, 152, *153*
    Skinny Cookie 2.0, *210*, 211
peanuts, in Kelp Noodle Salad with Almond Ginger Dressing, 138, *139*
peas, in Triple Goddess Soup, *150*, 151
pecans
    Banana Bread Superfood Granola, 96, *97*
    Best Banana Bread, 220
peppermint tea, in Digestive Tincture, 57, *57*
Pesto, Classic, 190
Pickled Vegetables, Quick and Easy, 186, *187*
pineapple

Street Beet Burger, *130*, 162–163, *163*

nut butters, pantry essentials, 33
nut milk bags, 36
nutritional yeast, 177
nuts, pantry essentials, 31

    Summer Peach Crumble, *238*, 239
    Sweet Potato Porridge, 103
oils, pantry essentials, 31–32
oranges
    Creamsicle Clementine Chia Pudding, 104, *105*
    Detox Juice, 54, *55*
    Wild Blueberry Chia Jam, *110*, 111
Our Famous Brazil Nut Parmesan, 198
Oven-Roasted Tomatoes, *188*, 189
overnight oats, 27

    Cauliflower Pizza, *154*, 155–156
    Detox Juice, 54, *55*
    Pura Vida Smoothie, 81
    Simple Green, *62*, 63
    Wake-Up Tonic, 47
Pizza, Cauliflower, *154*, 155–156
plant-based alternatives, pantry essentials, 33
Polenta with Oven-Roasted Tomatoes, Kale, and Mushrooms, 158, *159*
Popcorn, Movie Night, 182, *183*
potatoes, in Easy Cheese Sauce, 194
pretzels, in Compost Cookies, 213
probiotic capsules, in Coconut Yogurt, 112
pumpkin
    Creamy Pumpkin Mac 'n' Cheese, *160*, 161
    Pumpkin Waffles, *118*, 119–120
    Sugar Cookies with Pumpkin Frosting, *204*, 205–206
pumpkin seeds
    about, *128*
    Compost Cookies, 213
    Fat Bombs, *114*, 115
    Loaded Lentil Salad, *140*, 141
Pura Vida Smoothie, 81

Q

Quick and Easy Pickled Vegetables, 186, *187*
quinoa
    about, 27
    Buddha Bowl 2.0, *132*, 133

R

rapini, in Cauliflower Steaks with Cashew Butter Kimchi Sauce and Grilled Rapini, 169–170, *171*
Raspberry Cloud Chia Pudding, 116
Raw Date Sauce, 244
refried black beans, in Friday Night Dip, *184*, 185
reishi mushrooms
    about, 27
    Supernatural Cacao "Coffee," 48, *49*
rice noodles, in Pad Thai, 152, *153*
Roasted Beet Hummus, *192*, 193
roots, pantry essentials, 33

S

salad dressings
    Almond Ginger Dressing, 196
    Lemon Tahini Dressing, 197
salads
    Chopped Kale Power Salad, *136*, 137
    Kelp Noodle Salad with Almond Ginger Dressing, 138, *139*
    Loaded Lentil Salad, *140*, 141
    Warm Cauliflower Salad, 142, *143*
Sandwich, B.L.A.T., 166, *167*
sauces
    Cacao Sauce, 246
    Easy Cheese Sauce, 194
    Kimchi Cashew Butter Sauce, *168*, 170, *171*
    Raw Date Sauce, 244
    Turmeric Miso Sauce, 196
Savory Breakfast Bowl, *122*, 123
seed butters, pantry essentials, 33
seeds, pantry essentials, 31
sesame seeds
    about, 28
    Kelp Noodle Salad with Almond Ginger Dressing, 138, *139*
shiitake mushrooms, in Gut Healing Broth, *144*, 145
shikimate, 28
shortbread
    Indulgent Shortbread Cookies, 214, *215*
    Lemony Shortbread Cookies, 214
    Matcha Shortbread, *216*, 217
Shortcake, Strawberry, 236, *237*
Simple Green, *62*, 63
Street Beet Burger, *130*, 162–163, *163*
Sweet Potato Porridge, 103
Simple Vanilla Buttercream, 243
skillets, 36
Skinny Cookie 2.0, *210*, 211
smoothie bowls
    Eternal Glow Bowl, 88, *89*
    Green Goddess Smoothie Bowl, *90*, 91
    Mermaid Bowl, 92, *93*
smoothies
    Date Shake, 76, *77*
    Golden Mylkshake, 79
    Hormone Balancing Smoothie, 80
    Palm Springs Smoothie, 86, *87*
    Pura Vida Smoothie, 81
    Sunrise Smoothie, 82, *83*
    Sweet Potato Smoothie, *84*, 85
S'mores Cupcakes, *226*, 227
snacks
    Carrot Bacon, 174, *175*
    Crispy Baked Chickpeas, 178, *179*
    Eazy Cheezy Kale Chips, *176*, 177
    Movie Night Popcorn, 182, *183*
Soul-Soothing Turmeric Tonic, *56*, *66*, 67
soups
    Gut Healing Broth, *144*, 145
    Sweet Roasted Corn Soup, *148*, 149
    Triple Goddess Soup, *150*, 151
    Warming Squash and Carrot Soup, 146, *147*
spices, pantry essentials, 32
spinach
    Buddha Bowl 2.0, *132*, 133
    Cauliflower Pizza, *154*, 155–156

Green Goddess Smoothie Bowl, *90*, 91
Gut Healing Broth, *144*, 145
Palm Springs Smoothie, 86, *87*
Simple Green, *62*, 63
Triple Goddess Soup, *150*, 151
Warm Cauliflower Salad, 142, *143*
spiralizers, 36
spirulina
    about, 27
    Mermaid Bowl, 92, *93*
    Palm Springs Smoothie, 86, *87*
Squash and Carrot Soup, 146, *147*
strawberries
    Raspberry Cloud Chia Pudding, 116
    Strawberry Shortcake, 236, *237*
Street Beet Burger, *130*, 162–163, *163*
Sucanat, *200*, 221
sugar, *201*
Sugar Cookies with Pumpkin Frosting, *204*, 205–206
Sugar-Free Frosting, 245
Summer Peach Crumble, *238*, 239
summer squash, in Quick and Easy Pickled Vegetables, 186
sunflower seed butter

Chocolate Chunk Turmeric Cookies, *218*, 219
Skinny Cookie 2.0, *210*, 211
sunflower seeds
    about, 27–28
    Classic Pesto, 190–191
    Eazy Cheezy Kale Chips, *176*, 177
Sunrise Smoothie, 82, *83*
superfoods, 20–28, 80
Supernatural Cacao "Coffee," 48, *49*
sweet potato and buckwheat noodles, in Pad Thai, 152, *153*
sweet potatoes
    Chopped Kale Power Salad, *136*, 137
    Eternal Glow Bowl, 88, *89*
    Loaded Lentil Salad, *140*, 141
    Magical Chocolate Birthday Cake, *232*, 233
    puree, *201*
    Sweet Potato Nachos, *164*, 165
    Sweet Potato Porridge, 103
    Sweet Potato Smoothie, *84*, 85
    Sweet Potato Toasts, *108*, *109*
Sweet Roasted Corn Soup, *148*, 149
sweeteners, pantry essentials, 32–33, *200–201*

T

tahini
    about, 28
    Kimchi Cashew Butter Sauce, *168*, 170, *171*
    Lemon Tahini Dressing, 197
    Roasted Beet Hummus, *192*, 193
    Turmeric Miso Sauce, 196
tempeh, in Pad Thai, 152–153, *153*
Thai red curry paste, in Warming Squash and Carrot Soup, 146, *147*
Tincture, Digestive, 56–57
toasts
    Sweet Potato Toasts, 108, *109*
    Toasts with Avocado, 124, *125–126*, 127
tomatoes
    B.L.A.T. Sandwich, 166, *167*
    Creamy Polenta with Oven-Roasted Tomatoes, Kale, and Mushrooms, 158, *159*
    Friday Night Dip, *184*, 185
    Guac and Chips, *180*, 181
    Oven-Roasted Tomatoes, *188*, 189

    Savory Breakfast Bowl, *122*, 123
    Toasts with Avocado, *126*, 127
tonics
    Soul-Soothing Turmeric Tonic, *56*, *66*, 67
    Wake-Up Tonic, 47
    Wellness Shot, 68, *69*
tools, 36
Triple Goddess Soup, *150*, 151
turmeric
    about, 28, *41*, 67, *89*
    Choco Bowl, *98*, 99
    Chocolate Chunk Turmeric Cookies, *218*, 219
    Detox Juice, 54, *55*
    Eternal Glow Bowl, 88, *89*
    Golden Mylkshake, 79
    Pura Vida Smoothie, 81
    Savory Breakfast Bowl, *122*, 123
    Soul-Soothing Turmeric Tonic, *56*, *66*, 67
    Turmeric Miso Sauce, 196
    Wake-Up Tonic, 47

V

vegetables
- Gut Healing Broth, *144*, 145
- pantry essentials, 33

W

Waffles, Pumpkin, *118*, 119–120
wakame seaweed, in Gut Healing Broth, *144*, 145
Wake-Up Tonic, 47
walnuts
- about, *129*
- Banana Bread Superfood Granola, 96, *97*
- Best Banana Bread, 220
- Kelly and Erinn's Superfood Raw-Nola, 100, *101*
- Street Beet Burger, *130*, 162–163, *163*
- Summer Peach Crumble, *238*, 239

Warm Cauliflower Salad, 142, *143*

Y

Yogurt, Coconut, 112

Z

zucchinis, in Curly Green Bowl, 134, *135*

Quick and Easy Pickled Vegetables, 186
vinegars, pantry essentials, 31–32

Warming Squash and Carrot Soup, 146, *147*
Wellness Shot, 68, *69*
Whipped Cream, 242
White Pine Needle Tea, *56*, 71
white pine needle tincture
- about, 28, 71
- Soul-Soothing Turmeric Tonic, *56*, *66*, 67

wild blueberries
- about, 28
- Wild Blueberry Chia Jam, 111

William, Anthony, 64

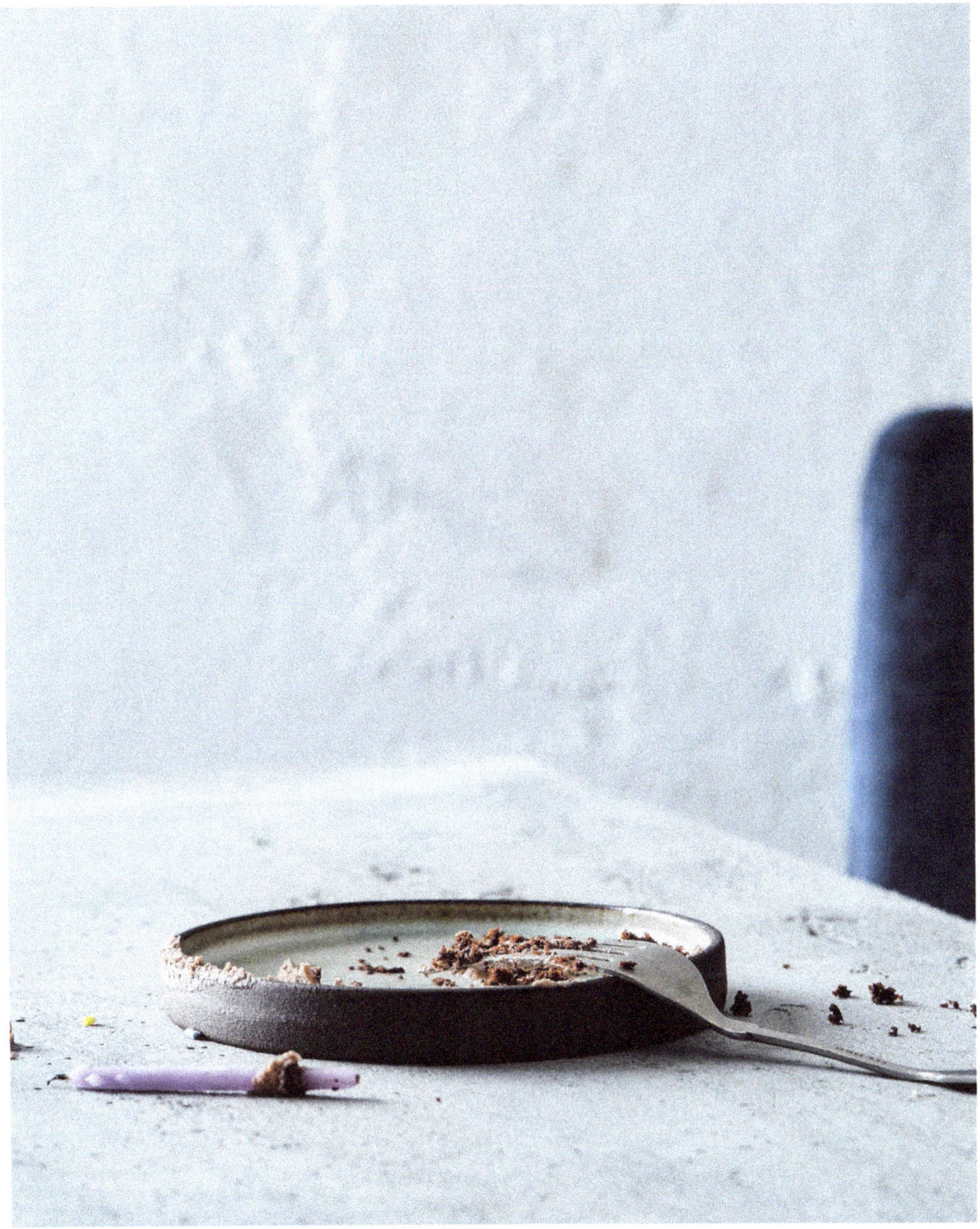

Printed in the USA
CPSIA information can be obtained
at www.ICGtesting.com
LVHW071557270924
792327LV00013B/268

9 781039 137400